CW01368435

Blade Runner: The Inside Story

BLADE RUNNER: THE INSIDE STORY
ISBN 1 84023 210 2

Published by
Titan Books
A division of
Titan Publishing Group Ltd
144 Southwark St
London
SE1 0UP

First edition November 2000
10 9 8 7 6 5

Blade Runner: The Inside Story © 2000 Don Shay. All rights reserved.

Blade Runner photographs © 1982 by Warner Brothers and The Blade Runner Partnership. All rights reserved. Special effects unit still photography by Virgil Mirano. Additional photography by Mark Stetson and Bill George. All photographs are reproduced for the purposes of review or criticism within 'fair dealing' requirements.

Don Shay has asserted his right to be identified as Author of this Work, in accordance with the Copyright, Designs and Patents Act, 1988.

Special thanks to Jeff Walker. The publishers would like to thank Don Shay and Douglas Trumbull for their help with this project.

The contents of this book were originally published in 1982 as *Cinefex* issue 9. Please contact www.cinefex.com for current subscription details.

What did you think of this book? We love to hear from our readers. Please e-mail us at: readerfeedback@titanemail.com or write to Reader Feedback at the address above.

No part of this publication may be reproduced, stored in a retrieval system, or transmitted, in any form or by any means without the prior written permission of the publisher, nor be otherwise circulated in any form of binding or cover other than that in which it is published and without a similar condition being imposed on the subsequent purchaser.

A CIP catalogue record for this title is available from the British Library.

Printed in China

Blade Runner: The Inside Story

Don Shay

cinefex
Titan Books

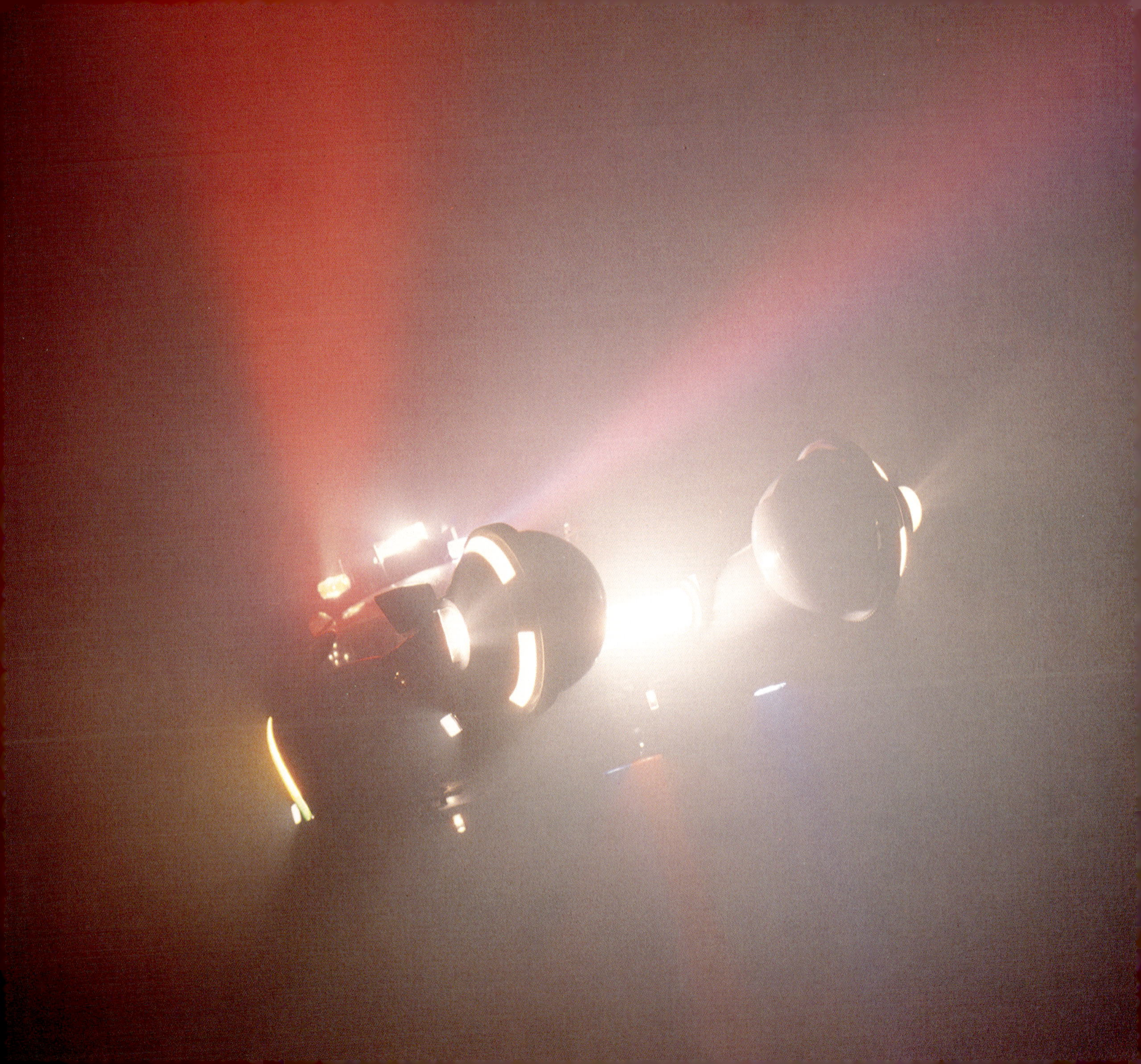

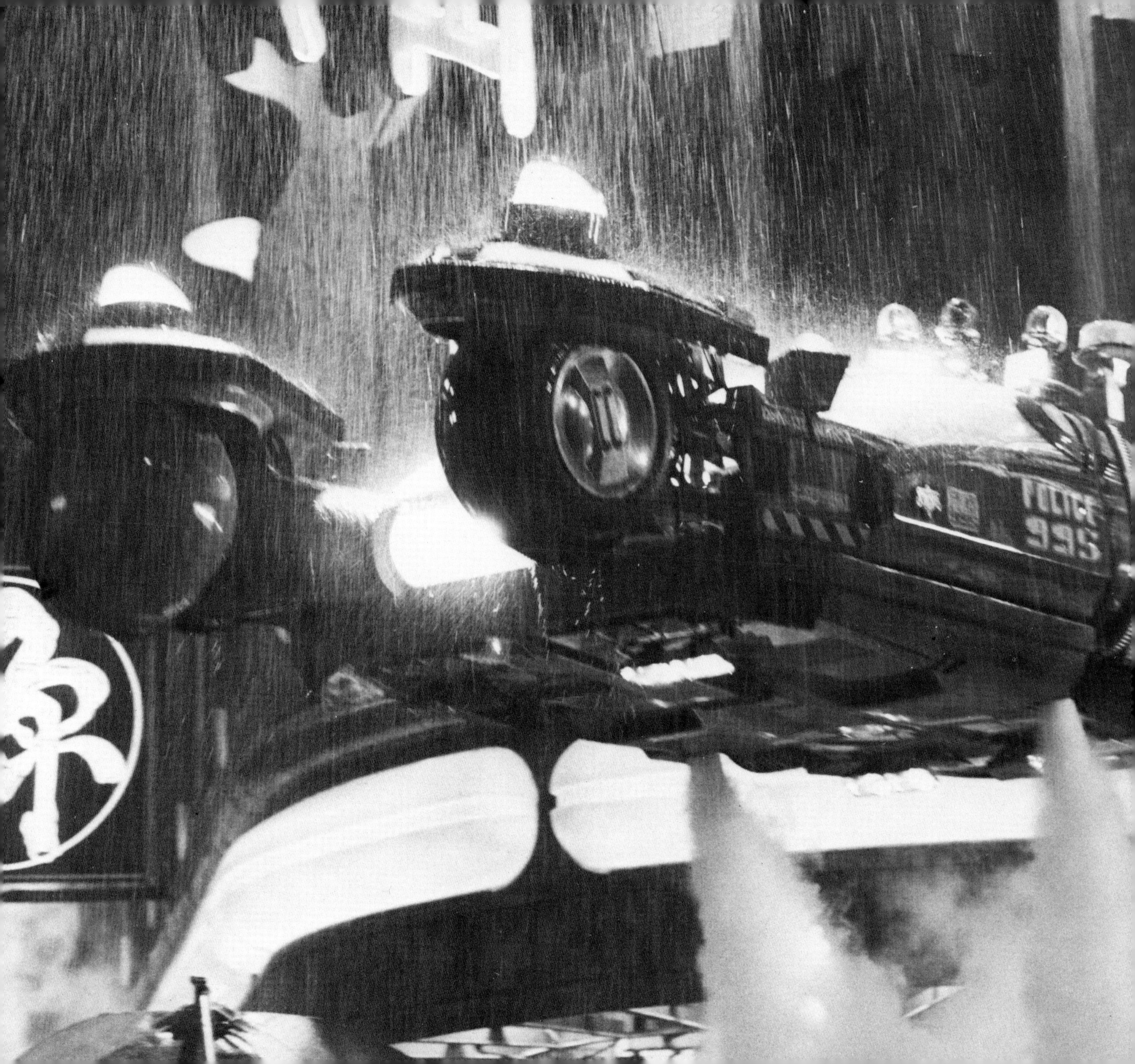
POLICE
995

cinefex

...the journal of cinematic illusions

editor & publisher
Don Shay

contributing editors
Paul Mandell
Jordan Fox

circulation manager
JoDyne Shay

editorial consultant
Robert P. Everett

editorial services
Ann Dredla

CINEFEX 9 — July 1982. Published quarterly at P.O. Box 20027, Riverside, California 92516. Subscription rates (U.S. only): four issues – $12; ten issues – $25. Return postage must accompany all unsolicited manuscripts, photos or other materials. Printed by R.B. Graphics, Riverside, California; typesetting by The Set-Up, Riverside, California; color separations by ViviColour, Covina, California. Contents copyright © 1982 by Don Shay. All rights reserved. Reproduction in whole or in part without permission is prohibited.

Blade Runner — 2020 Foresight 4

After more than a year of intensive labor, the visual effects craftsmen at Entertainment Effects Group have produced the definitive urban future for *Blade Runner* — Ridley Scott's stylish homage to *film noir*. A polluted, overpopulated megalopolis, the *Blade Runner* city was created largely with miniatures and matte paintings — and effects supervisors Douglas Trumbull, Richard Yuricich and David Dryer detail the arduous process by which it was generated and captured on film. On a broader scale, director Ridley Scott and design consultant Syd Mead discuss the evolution of the project and the philosophy behind its distinctive ambience. Adding further dimension are director of miniature photography Dave Stewart and cameraman Don Baker, matte painters Matthew Yuricich and Rocco Gioffre, designer Tom Cranham, model shop supervisors Mark Stetson and Wayne Smith and modelmaker Bill George, animation supervisor John Wash and cameraman Glenn Campbell, Compsy tech director Richard Hollander, optical supervisor Robert Hall, matte cameraman Robert Bailey, still photographer Virgil Mirano, lab liaison Jack Hinkle and effects auditor Diana Gold. Together, they present one of the most thorough accounts ever of a major special effects project — covering the design, construction and photography of the massive Tyrell pyramids, the vast Hades wasteland, the extended cityscapes and the wondrous flying vehicles. *Article by Don Shay.*

FRONT COVER — A police spinner slices through the skies in *Blade Runner*.
A giant advertising blimp drifts above the *Blade Runner* city — BACK COVER.

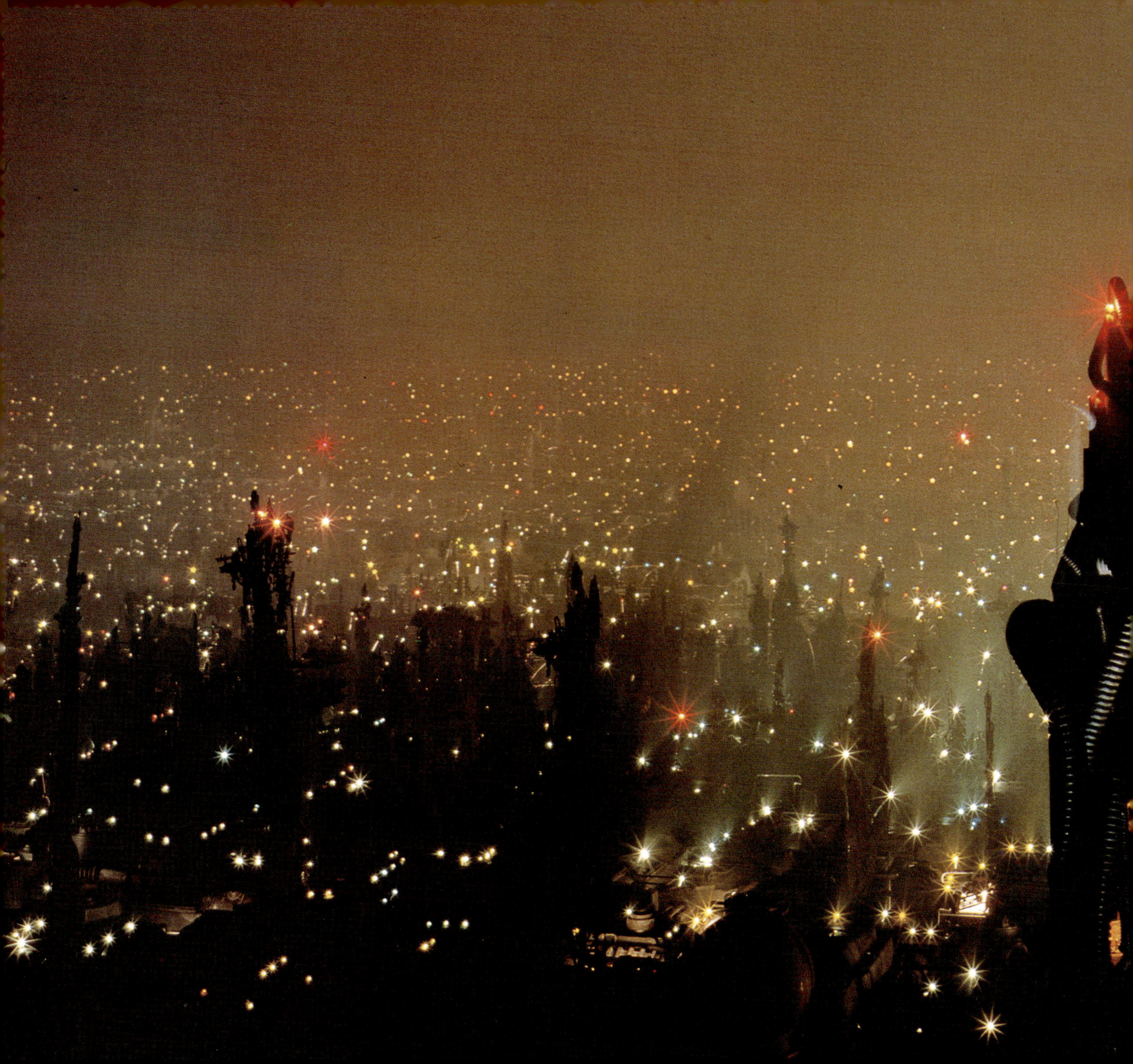

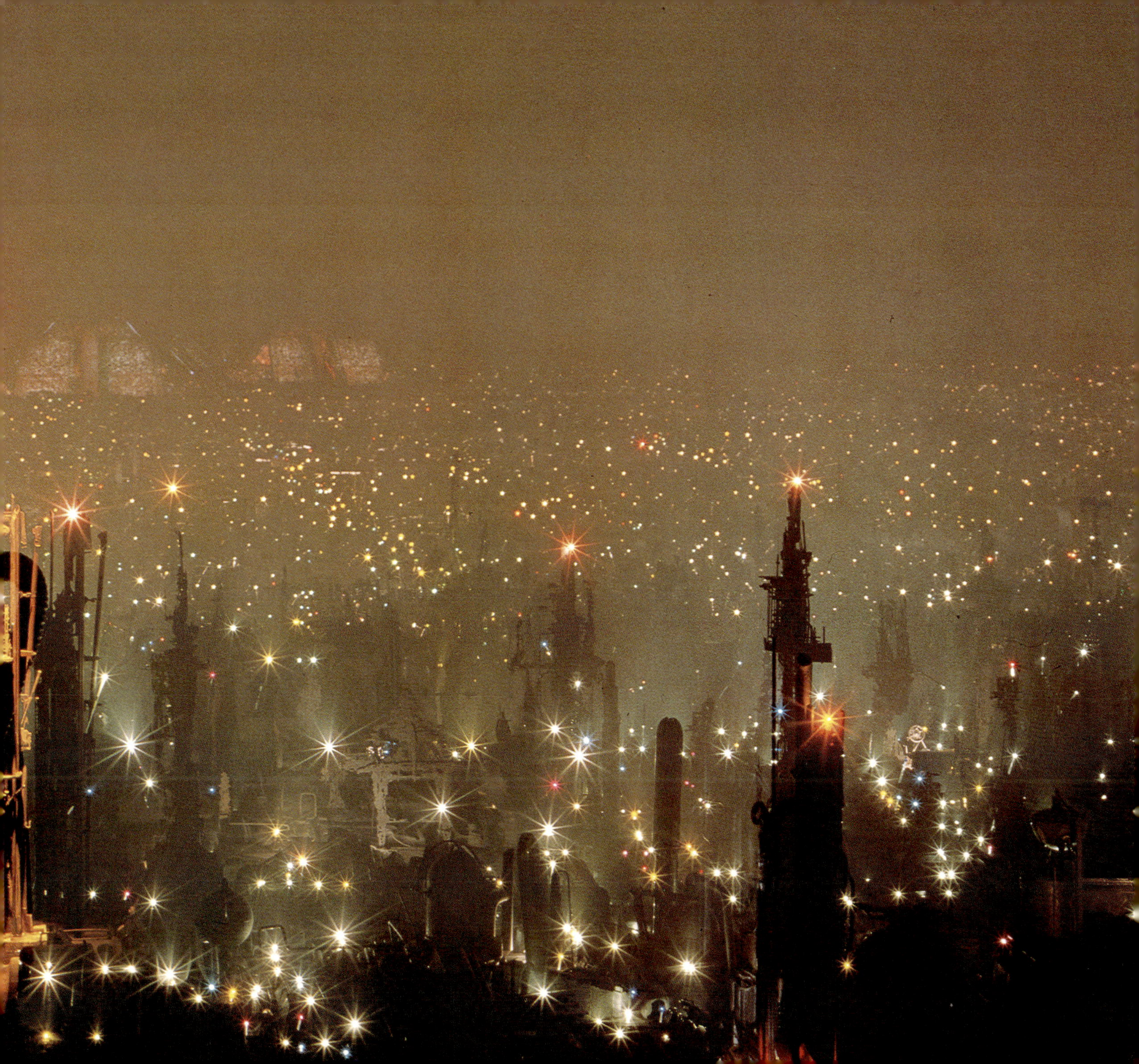

Four desperate fugitives...twenty-three brutal murders...a former super-cop mustered out of retirement... If the ingredients of *Blade Runner* seem vaguely familiar, it is only because they have formed the basis for a whole subgenre of movie melodramas stretching back a half-century or more. What sets *Blade Runner* clearly apart, however, is the stage upon which these familiar elements have been played. The year is 2020. The place — an unspecified magalopolis blighted by the mutually-reinforcing pestilence of overpopulation and pollution. Four replicants — genetically engineered humanoids developed for off-world warfare and slave labor — have hijacked a shuttle, returned illegally to earth, and infiltrated the sprawling city. Veteran blade runner Rick Deckard — played by Harrison Ford — is assigned the difficult task of identifying and exterminating the renegade quasi-humans.

In the afterglow of his phenomenal success with *Alien*, director Ridley Scott had been engaged by Dino De Laurentiis to apply his highly-individualized expertise to the oft-abandoned *Dune* project. A year later, however, the script had still not developed into something Scott considered filmable; so he shifted over to *Blade Runner*, which was being produced by Michael Deeley for Filmways Pictures. *Blade Runner*'s passage to the screen was to prove almost as convoluted as its plot when Filmways began buckling under the weight of financial overextension and decided to jettison the $15 million production only a couple of months before principal photography was to begin. Deeley, however, was able to turn the project around, and less than two weeks later *Blade Runner* was regenerated on The Burbank Studios lot under a complex financial infrastructure involving The Ladd Company, Tandem Productions and Warner Brothers. Meanwhile, the preproduction effort proceeded virtually unaltered.

From the start, the urban environment set forth in the film had been one of Ridley Scott's primary concerns. "I came in on the project after the first screenplay had been written — or after the first presentable screenplay had been written, so who knows how many other drafts had been done before then. But as a result, the indications by the writer about what the city was like, what the world was like, and what the environment was like, were already in there — but it was really beyond description. From there to the point of how you actually carry it out is a long, long road. And mainly that was cooked up by designers and illustrators and effects people. That's always the final interpretation of any screenplay."

Blade Runner represents a significant departure from the novel upon which it was based — Philip K. Dick's *Do Androids Dream of Electric Sheep?* — not only in terms of plot structure, but also in terms of environment. Dick foresaw a post-holocaust world in which most of the planet's animal life had become extinct and in which the great population centers had atrophied in the wake of widespread off-world emigration. The city as put forth in the film, however, is teeming with life — an overabundance of life, in fact.

"The city we present is overkill," Ridley Scott admitted, "but I always get the impression of New York as being overkill. You go into New York on a bad day and you look around and you feel this place is going to grind to a halt any minute — which it nearly does all too often. All you need is a garbage strike or a subway strike or an electrical blowout and you have absolute chaos. So we took that idea and projected it forty years into the future and came up with a megalopolis — the kind of city that could be where New York and Chicago join, with maybe a hundred million people living there. Or maybe San Francisco and Los Angeles. In fact, at one point we were going to call the city San Angeles, which would of course have suggested that the eight-hundred-mile-long western seaboard had been transformed into a single population center with giant cities and monolithic buildings at either end and then this strange kind of awful suburb in the middle. I thought the idea was interesting, but the city's now been moved to the East Coast because it's raining so much.

"Anyway, it seemed to me that in such a proscenium there would be a lot of air traffic. I picked that up from the fact that I used to fly in and out of New York a lot over a period of about five years, back before they stopped the helicopters landing on top of the Pan American Building. It was seven minutes from the airport to the roof, and I could remember coming in in January or February — in blizzards and high winds — and landing on the Pan Am Building. We used to drift in over the city, very close to the buildings, and it *felt* like the way of the future. Ultimately, they stopped it. There was a crash of some sort and they decided it was totally unsafe. But when we started working on this film, it seemed logical to me that there'd be a lot of air traffic — probably with a hands-off fail-safe system of some sort — and every building would have a landing platform on its roof. Forty years may be a bit soon for that, but if someone had projected in 1910 — or whenever it was the first Model T was built — that you'd come into the office every morning with ten thousand other cars driving fifty-five miles an hour, fifteen feet apart, you'd probably have said, 'You're fuckin' crazy!' So, from there to some future city where the World Trade Center might be half the size of some other buildings, and where rotorless jump-jet platforms are on every rooftop, is not terribly far-fetched. In fact, it's a totally logical process the way the world's going now. I don't suppose there are going to be housewives flying around Manhattan for a long time, but I would think very soon they will get back to the idea of that original Pan American helicopter. So we proceeded in that direction. The first vehicles would be police. The police, by then, will be paramilitary — they're already paramilitary in Los Angeles. Then there'd be corporate and other official vehicles, and already you'd be creating a helluva traffic jam in the air. But we all agreed and felt that that was pretty much the way the cities will go. And also, for us, it was a very nice visual notion."

It was, in fact, the visual potential inherent in the project that Ridley Scott found most intriguing. And so, while the script went through a series of progressive rewrites — first by Hampton Fancher and later by David W. Peoples — Ridley Scott turned his primary attention to the overall look of the film. "Before I bring a production designer in — no matter what the genre we're going to be attempting — I like to involve a conceptual illustrator or two. Just to get the ideas flowing. It was a process that worked very well for me on *Alien* when I chose H.R. Giger and Ron Cobb — two people who were totally steeped in that area of thinking — and had them develop a lot of the designs. Most good production designers can do things within their own experience very well — or within the realm of their own references, which could be books or whatever. But to take a film production designer and expect him to project himself — on the level that *I* want — into a period which takes us forty to sixty years into the future is unlikely. And so, because I knew I was touching 'near future,' the logical thing to do was try to find a good industrial designer, who was probably working on projections already anyway. About three years ago, I bought a book called *Sentinel*, which was Syd Mead's book and which was really very interesting because it had *very* exotic projections about vehicles and industrial design — done for everybody from General Motors to washing machine companies to computer manufacturers. What I especially liked was the fact that Syd Mead's future seemed to be well-grounded in logic, and that's what I wanted for *Blade Runner*. I wanted it to be futuristic without being silly."

"Originally I was hired to do six vehicle types for the movie," Mead revealed. "And from the very first meeting we definitely knew that we wanted a flying car — which in the script was called a spinner. So I thought to myself that if we want a flying car, we wouldn't want folding wings or a lot of complicated parts that folded out or collapsed back in. It had to be a self-contained, car-sized thing. I knew about an enclosed lift system called an aerodyne, which is the basic principal of the Harrier vertical takeoff jet aircraft the British have. The aerodyne allows you to produce lift internally, without wings or anything at all; and while the Harrier *does* in fact have wings for forward flight, in the case of the car, we were going to pretend that you could generate all controlled lift internally and vent it out through the bottom. So that was the start of the idea. We wanted a sort of a clean shape that could roll along the ground on wheels and blend with traffic; but we also wanted a shape that looked like it would do what it was supposed to do — which is fly. That's why we had the enclosed smooth back, because we needed some deflection to funnel the thrust down when you're taking off and landing. And the forward part of the car had the wheels suspended out in front for much the same reason, so you could direct and deflect the airstream forward and up and down, and not have the whole front end of the car in front of all that. So it was basically an industrial design approach to the problem.

"After I'd done some initial idea sketches, I brought them back and went over them with Ridley, and he thought they were too sleek. Actually, I felt that way, too; but I thought the logical way to go about it would be to design the vehicles as if they would be normal vehicles — consumer items — so you'd start off with a very logical, real-looking piece of machinery. Then the next stage would be to load it up with some more stuff so it didn't

Entertainment Effects Group partners Richard Yuricich and Douglas Trumbull first worked together on 2001: A Space Odyssey. *In subsequent years, their professional association extended through such landmark effects films as* Silent Running, Close Encounters of the Third Kind *and* Star Trek – The Motion Picture — *and at the time they were approached to do* Blade Runner, *both men were already involved in preproduction on* Brainstorm. *They agreed, however, to take on the Blade Runner assignment, get it up and running, and then turn the supervisory reins over to a designated representative.*

look too clean. So as time went on, we gradually degraded the original design by overlaying bits of equipment and things to roughen up the texture. It's like if you see early renderings from Northrop or Lockheed on their jet fighter concepts, they're very, very sleek vehicles. Then as they run them through tests — static tests and wind tunnels and actual in-field use — they'll start altering the intake area or adding antenna attachments or maybe airstream deflectors. But it'll change as it goes through, and I wanted to end up with that kind of added-on detail look. If you think back at what happened to the VW Bug over all the years it was in production, you'll recall the incredible configurations that were done with that vehicle as a basic unit. And I had that in mind as sort of a guiding theory of how the vehicles should end up looking."

The strictly functional retrofitted approach first applied to the *Blade Runner* vehicle designs would ultimately color the rest of the film as well. "The social theory," Mead continued, "was that the consumer delivery system had become interrupted, and the larger energies in the system were being collected at the top by big corporate conglomerates and were being syphoned off into off-world explorations. As a result, the capital delivery system to the populace was short-circuited. So if you had a car, you'd just have to keep it working. As the cities and air become more dense, you might have to buy new lighting packages, or another air conditioner that would go on the roof, or heavy-duty windshield wipers — all sorts of after-market equipment, which you always get anyway. So we just took all the trends in progress in those selected departments and accelerated them. That's why the cars look sort of lumpy, and they have strange lights and attachments and graphics: 'This car is monitored. Do not tamper — you will be electrocuted.' But if you took off this added surface detail — the light racks and all this stuff — it would be a very streamlined, very sleek vehicle. And that made it real — which is very important. When you're creating an artificial reality, you can't get too far-out. You have to do what the audience believes is probably the way things would look. All the elements have to look like they belong where they are, and they have to explain themselves as they flash by. Otherwise it doesn't work, and it puts a roadblock in the way of the story.

"When I'm designing, it's hard for me to think of an object as floating in isolation. If it's a car, it has to be on a street, with some background detail so it looks like it belongs where it's eventually going to be used. So in the process of doing some Tempera sketches for Ridley to look at, I also put in background indications. I'd read the script, and I'd been at meetings where Ridley and the others were discussing the feeling they were after. So I started putting in background elements that I thought would help the idea along so they could not only just evaluate the vehicle design, but also see how it might fit into the visual atmosphere we were creating as we went along. Ridley liked some of my ideas, so he said: 'Why don't you take the New York street at The Burbank Studios and photograph it and see what you can do with this retrofit technique?'"

Thus, working directly over photographs of the existing structures and facades on the old backlot — and applying his customarily acute sense of functional rationale — Syd Mead prepared detailed watercolor renderings of the future he perceived to be in Ridley Scott's mind. "The idea was that basically it was going to be unpleasant to be at street level in the cities. The old city structures would still be there, but the buildings might now be hollowed out and used as service access or plenum chambers for the really big megastructures above them. Or maybe the building would be left where it was, but with a whole column built inside; so you'd have a normal five-story building, and then out of the top of it would be a big pylon that would go up a hundred stories to the underside of another building. So there'd be all this incredible changing scale. And I don't think it's too farfetched. If today we can build the World Trade Center, which is two buildings, side-by-side, about eleven hundred feet tall, it seems reasonable to assume that forty years into the future — with better steels and technology and computerized wind loading and such — we could probably at least triple that as a fairly common occurrence. And it's also reasonable to assume that if that happens, the older sections of the city — those closest to the ground — will be the least desirable for living and working.

"So I thought, if it's unpleasant to look out the window, with flat-screen TV — which is realizable right now; it's just not on the market — you'd rent a service that would come and put a box outside your window and you could have Niagara Falls or snow-capped mountains or whatever, complete with sound and motion. And you'd end up with a residential urban area that looks sort of like a warehouse district because there's all these funny boxes and things on the outsides of buildings. Ridley thought it was really kind of a neat idea because it produced a strange, uninhabitable look, but at the same time there was light activity — little flashes coming out from the match lines, and all. So that started my involvement with doing the street sets.

"The other thing was that the street sets were going to show this accumulated progress. The buildings would just become surfaces on which you'd mount retrofitted electrical conduits, air conditioning ducts and all kinds of other things. Additional power would come from a generator sitting on the street — which might be there for years, but initially it was a temporary idea. And then these big cables would be running up the sides of all the buildings. But essentially it was an industrial design approach, because there had to be a very solid, mechanical logic behind it. It had to look like what it was. And what it was was a city whose discreet individual structures had been enveloped into sort of an urban machine, with people living inside." Once approved, the basic street designs were turned over to production designer Lawrence G. Paull, who handled the difficult transition from concept to reality. "My ideas — a lot of them — went through practically unchanged," Mead marveled. "In fact, it was spooky walking around that backlot set and seeing some buildings that were right off my Tempera sketch." At Ridley Scott's continued instigation, Mead transitioned next into some of the

Harrison Ford stars as Rick Deckard, a seasoned bounty hunter highly skilled in the art of identifying and exterminating renegade replicants — genetically engineered beings who sometimes rebel against their demeaning station in life and try to assimilate themselves into human society. / Director Ridley Scott confers with Douglas Trumbull on the set. An EEG supervisor was always on hand during any live-action sequence requiring later optical enhancement. / Scott discusses a matte painting concept with futuristic designer Syd Mead and effects supervisor David Dryer. Dryer took over for Trumbull and Yuricich midway through principal photography and saw the project through to completion.

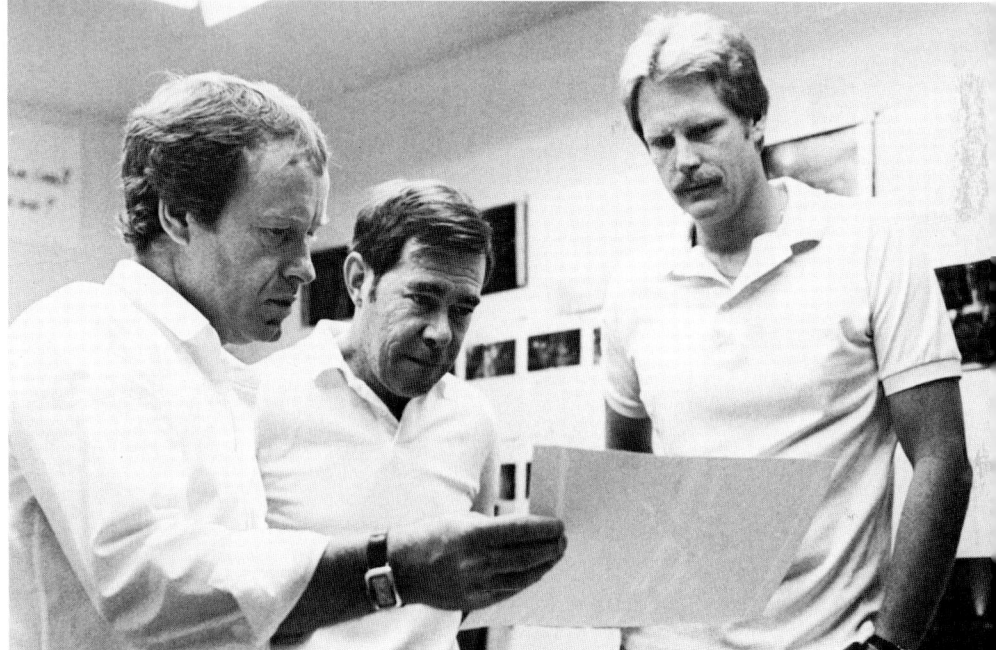

CINEFEX 9 ▶ 9

interior set design and eventually went on to devise most of the film's highly distinctive props and fixtures.

It was clear right from the start, though, that *Blade Runner* would require more than a retrofitted backlot street to suggest the scope of the megalopolis Ridley Scott and Syd Mead were envisioning. Miniatures and matte paintings would be required at a minimum, and they needed to be of the highest quality if they were to meet the increasingly difficult challenge of suspending audience disbelief. With high ambitions — but limited funding — Scott and his associates visited the industry's most prominent effects facilities and solicited bids from those they considered most likely. "There are many effects houses in the United States," said Scott, "but really it narrows down to about three groups — Trumbull's, Lucas' and Dykstra's. And I always wanted to work with Doug Trumbull, because I guess I admire his stuff more than anybody else's. Doug is kind of a scientist really, and an innovator. And he's a director, so you're already fourteen steps ahead on an understanding level."

Douglas Trumbull was not exactly free and clear to take on the assignment, however. After *Star Trek – The Motion Picture*, Trumbull's contractual obligations to Paramount came to a close, and the studio shuttered the effects facility in Venice and sold off all the equipment which did not specifically belong to Trumbull or his associate, Richard Yuricich. Trumbull, in the meantime, had placed his own personal project — *Brainstorm* — with Metro-Goldwyn-Mayer. Nevertheless, the *Blade Runner* assignment had considerable appeal — both from an aesthetic and a pragmatic point of view.

"One of the first things that appealed to me about the project," said Trumbull, "was that it was *not* a space movie. I'm just real tired of doing spaceships against star backgrounds. I was also very impressed with Ridley Scott and his ability to express himself, as well as his ability to draw while he's trying to describe something. Plus the fact he had already come off *Alien* and had had a lot of experience with television commercials — which is really a great trial by fire, because commercials tend to be full of effects and camera problems and unique lenses and all that kind of stuff. And then, too, they came to us early enough so we could really plan in advance what their needs would be, and solve a lot of the problems, build miniatures, and get a lot of work done before principal photography. In fact, we had never done a film before where we were able to get as deeply into the effects prior to principal photography as we did on *Blade Runner*. So I just felt that the whole project had a lot of components going for it. The one hitch, of course, was that Dick Yuricich and I were in a transition phase from just being special effects contractors to Dick being the director of photography and I being the director on *Brainstorm*. So we told them in advance that Dick and I would design all the general approaches to solving their problems and build all the appropriate equipment, and in essence just try and solve all the problems up front and try to make it into sort of a manufacturing operation that could then be taken over by somebody we would designate."

Although he would not be called upon for several more months, the individual selected by Trumbull and Yuricich to take charge in their absence was David Dryer. Dryer, a Phi Beta Kappa graduate of the University of Southern California film school, had no feature film experience, but had extensive background as a documentary film editor and a director of television commercials. In the early Seventies, Richard Yuricich had served as assistant to Dryer's regular cameraman on a number of commercials produced at EUE/Screen Gems, and Yuricich was impressed with the young director's creativity and technical expertise. The two men had kept in touch over the years, and when *Blade Runner* presented the need for supervisory reinforcement, both Trumbull and Yuricich were in concurrence that David Dryer would be an ideal candidate.

The midstream managerial changeover was acceptable to the *Blade Runner* organization, but another major obstacle was still in place. "When we budgeted the film originally," said Richard Yuricich, "it came in at $5.5 million. It wasn't storyboarded or anything at that point, but we were able to break the script down and take a broad swipe at it in terms of time and labor materials. Apogee came in at about the same figure. Some others, I understand, were even higher. The problem was that *Blade Runner* had only $2 million for effects, and that was it — period. Unfortunately, in this day and age, $2 million is a pretty limited budget." As it turned out, *Blade Runner*'s associate producer, Ivor Powell, was not only a longtime associate of Ridley Scott, but also an old friend of both Trumbull and Yuricich, dating back to *2001: A Space Odyssey* on which they had all worked. Together, the three hammered out a mutually advantageous agreement. The *Blade Runner* production company would take over the effects facility — which Trumbull and Yuricich had already leased back from Paramount as a preproduction base for *Brainstorm* — and put whatever effects personnel were needed directly on the *Blade Runner* payroll. A *Blade Runner* auditor would be on hand to coordinate between the effects and production staffs, and all expenditures would be monitored and approved by the backers. Since all expenses for personnel and materials were being borne by the parent company, there was no need for markup. What it made possible, though, was for Douglas Trumbull and Richard Yuricich to share time between *Blade Runner* and *Brainstorm* — and more importantly, allow them to reassemble their seasoned staff of regulars and keep them together through both projects. Even with the proposed arrangement, however, there was no way that $5.5 million worth of effects could be produced for $2 million. The script would have to be reworked.

One of the first things to go was an elaborate sequence which had been designed to introduce both Rick Deckard and the environment in which he operates. "We started originally on a train," Ridley Scott revealed, "coming in over this sort of desert landscape that was so bleak that — once again, like the city — you'd get the impression of overkill. The train is very sophisticated — a high-speed monorail that would do four hundred miles an hour — but despite its sleekness, it's still all plastered over with graffiti and shit. And except for Deckard — who's asleep — it's empty. From there we were going to follow the train into the city and then into the station — which was going to be Union Station in downtown Los Angeles, because I like that kind of funny architecture and I'm sure it'll still be here in forty years' time. Then he was going to get out of the train and into his own car. You don't know how long he's been away, but there's a thick coat of filth on it and he scrapes off the windshield with his credit card. He gets into the car and pulls out onto this massive sixteen-lane freeway, where he has to wait in a chute for a gap, and then a light bleeps on his dashboard and he funnels into this horrendous stream of traffic. From there, it's a hands-off thing. He sits back and picks up a newspaper as his car is taken into and through the city at a controlled speed of say forty miles an hour. Unless, of course, there's a traffic jam — which there just happens to be. A bleep comes through on the vidscreen inside his car and the guy at the other end says: 'Blade Runner One, where the hell have you been?' And he says: 'On holiday. Where have you been?' And so you learn a little bit about the character as he's being brought in. They want him to come to the precinct immediately, and he says he can't — he's on the Paxton ramp and there's a sixteen-lane traffic jam and he'll be at least two hours. So they tell him to abandon the vehicle and they'll pick him up. It's raining, but he does some button pushing and then just gets out of his car and starts jogging back through the traffic to a concrete tower which is supporting the freeway. The vehicle is on automatic; so when the traffic starts to move, it'll just be slid off the route and into the next available parking area. He goes up on top of this freeway tower and into a kind of concrete mushroom which is like a really small airport terminal, with plate glass all around it and all sorts of businessmen inside. Like the train, it's very sophisticated-looking, but all graffitied up and slushy — because it's snowing up there. Deckard gets himself a hot drink and sits down and continues reading his newspaper. Then he's bleeped on the intercom and he stands, throws his paper in the trash, dumps his cup of coffee and walks out through some glass doors onto this concrete lip which looks kind of like a platypus bill. A police spinner settles down on the ramp and Deckard runs across in the blizzard and climbs inside."

By the time the original script was fully revised, the anticipated number of effects shots had been reduced by well over half — split, more or less evenly, between reasonably straightforward matte paintings and some rather complex miniatures. Trumbull and Yuricich agreed that the work could be done within the allotted $2 million. "They wanted thirty-eight shots," Trumbull recalled. "At that point, they didn't know what the shots would be, but apparently *Alien* had had thirty-eight effects shots and so they had that for a frame of reference as to how many matte paintings and miniature shots they'd probably need to pull the story together. So they were specific in number, but not in content. Within those parameters, it was up to us to design and compose the shots, develop a storyboard that represented the shots, determine how big and to what scale the miniatures

An exterior and interior view of the spinner, designed and rendered by Syd Mead. The flying police cruiser was but one of a half-dozen distinctive vehicles Mead devised during his initial involvement with the film. As the project progressed, however, his responsibilities were broadened to include most of the exterior set design, plus a few interior concepts and numerous futuristic artifacts.

Standing amidst scavenged retrofitting materials, Syd Mead surveys the work in progress on The Burbank Studios backlot. / Ridley Scott's vision of the urban future was that the buildings of today would serve as the foundation from which truly massive structures — many times larger than anything currently in existence — would spring. At street level, the older buildings would still be present — retrofitted with cables and ducting and ablaze with garrish neon reflecting a projected shift in urban ethnic makeup. Syd Mead translated these ideas into detailed color renderings which served as bases for much of the set construction. / The historic, but now seldom-used, New York street set — reincarnated and projected forty years into the future for Blade Runner.

should be built, how many of them should be built, and then try to commit to a course of action that would get maximum utilization in the film and an absolute minimum of waste. And I think we really did a pretty good job. In terms of technique, though, it's all extrapolation from a lot of the things we worked out on *Close Encounters* using the smoke room, and *Star Trek* with a lot of flying vehicles and lens flares, and the optical compositing techniques we've developed and have used for a long time. Our *biggest* challenge, I think, was to develop a feeling of *immense* scale to the city — the idea of having something like New York with a lot of fifty or sixty story buildings that are part of the landscape; and then above that, these megastructures — as Ridley called them — huge structures that occupy several city blocks and go way, way up many hundreds of stories. And to get that sense of scale with a combination of matte paintings and miniatures, using buildings that you *know* the scale of in the foreground and megastructures behind them to throw them back but also make them look big — it's just not easy. In fact, it was one of our most difficult things — finding those funny blends of lighting and scale and aerial perspective to make it really look as big as Ridley wanted."

In the field of special effects, Douglas Trumbull and Richard Yuricich stand alone in their use of 65mm film stock for all composite work. Like VistaVision, 65mm provides an oversize frame area which tends to disguise the image degradation inherent in optical duping. Significantly, however, the 65mm frame is fifty percent larger overall than VistaVision, and in widescreen applications, has the added advantage of possessing nearly the same aspect ratio as the 35mm anamorphic production footage with which it is generally intercut. In the same application, the VistaVision frame must be cropped top and bottom, thereby sacrificing nearly thirty percent of its total image area. Over and above basic film format, Trumbull and Yuricich are likewise unique in their use of double- or multi-pass traveling mattes — as opposed to bluescreen — and in their employment of intermediate duping stock in their matte photography.

Formalizing their long-standing partnership under the name Entertainment Effects Group, Trumbull and Yuricich began gathering a core group of seasoned veterans for the *Blade Runner* project. As on both *Close Encounters* and *Star Trek*, Dave Stewart was engaged as director of miniature photography, Matthew Yuricich — Richard's older brother — was commissioned to execute the matte paintings, and Greg Jein was approached to supervise the model construction. Robert Hall, who had worked on *Close Encounters* but had subsequently joined the Universal Hartland team, would return to take charge of the optical department. While the remainder of the crew was being assembled, the facility — which had been stripped to the walls when Paramount pulled out — was being repartitioned and outfitted by engineering chief Evans Wetmore. Meanwhile, around the corner in a separate building, the model shop was coming together under the direction of Mark Stetson, who was filling in as Greg Jein's representative while Jein finished up his prior commitments to Francis Ford Coppola's *One From the Heart*.

One of the first, and most pressing, assignments for the effects unit was the design and construction of the Tyrell Corporation headquarters and its immediate surroundings. "Ridley didn't have a clear idea of whether it was a building out on the outskirts of town, or a big building right *in* town," Douglas Trumbull recalled, "and it didn't seem to resolve itself in the script. Frankly, I can't remember who came up with the idea, but we finally decided on a pair of pyramid-shaped buildings out in the middle of this vast sort of industrial landscape. Once that was decided, we had to get it together very, very rapidly, because they were about to start principal photography and the first scenes were scheduled for inside Tyrell's office — which was supposed to be near the top of one of the pyramids, and which had this great big office window that looked out over the other one. Since that was going to be done with front projection, we had to prepare the process plates right away." Trumbull called a meeting with designer-illustrator Tom Cranham, model shop supervisor Mark Stetson, plus a few others, and together they worked up a basic approach for the pyramid design. "The interior of the Tyrell office building was going to be this monolithic concrete-and-steel art deco style, and Larry Paull showed us some ideas and sketches for that. We used those as a basis for coming up with some of the exterior *detail* designs for the pyramid. For the basic structure, though, we decided to go after sort of a classic pyramid shape."

Tom Cranham was tasked with formulating a specific design for the pyramid. Cranham, during a fourteen-year association with producer Irwin Allen, had contributed storyboards and production illustrations for a string of disaster epics, ranging from *The Poseidon Adventure* and *The Towering Inferno* to such notedly lesser efforts as *The Swarm* and *When Time Ran Out*. During a subsequent preproduction stint on the initial *Buck Rogers* project, Cranham had occasion to meet Doug Trumbull; and a year or so later, when *Star Trek* came along, Trumbull hired him to assist in developing the Spock spacewalk blitz. Following that, Cranham spent two months in London as special assistant to Peter Hyams on *Outland*, contributing — uncredited — the initial designs for the film's shuttlecraft and illustrations of the Con-Am 27 exterior. His *Blade Runner* assignment was only slightly more down-to-earth. "Doug thought that a good starting point would be the Mayan pyramids in Mexico, in terms of a basic shape to work from. Architecturally, they're very interesting, because they have big massive blocks of stone, and in contrast they have these steps that run up the center so that the surface areas are broken up with different textures. They also have vertical runners that run up to the top, with gargoyle-type figures spaced along the way — which suggested to Doug that if you conceive of this pyramid as being a mile high, then the spots where the gargoyles were could perhaps be landing areas for spinners or helicopters or whatever else they chose. So that was the starting point, and I just went from there. One of the interesting design aspects, I thought, was the exterior elevators —

CINEFEX 9 ▶ 13

14 ◄ CINEFEX 9

which were huge and could carry massive amounts of cargo. I placed these in the area that corresponded to the stairs on the actual Mayan pyramids. So in essence, the elevators would take you up the side of the pyramid in much the same way that the Mayans used to go up on foot." Indeed, Cranham's final design — turned out in a matter of days — was remarkably faithful throughout to the ancient stone edifices on which it was modeled. What set it distinctively apart, however, were eight towering buttresses positioned in pairs around the base, slightly apart from the multi-tiered structure and cocked over at an angle corresponding to the pyramid's elevation. "The buttresses, I feel, were my great contribution. Without them, I think the pyramid would have been a much less interesting shape."

Once the basic concept was approved, Cranham prepared a detailed drawing which was then turned over to the model shop. By this time, less than a month remained before the start of principal photography, and the Tyrell office interiors were still slated for the first day's shooting. Convinced that the pyramid could not be completed in time for the initial front projection plates, Trumbull advised Ridley Scott and the producers of the fact, and assigned Matthew Yuricich to produce an appropriate painting which could be photographed and used instead. "Even though the overall shape was agreed upon fairly early," Cranham continued, "there was still the matter of the amount of detailing and what it should look like to make the pyramid a really fascinating-looking structure — detail-wise — over and above the basic shape. Doug kept impressing upon me that this building was supposed to be a mile high and that it had the mass of maybe a thousand Empire State Buildings, or more; and the detail had to be minutia personified, so that no matter how small we got the detail, we couldn't possibly make it too specific or too small. I ended up doing just reams and reams of thumbnail sketches of specific detail areas. Then I put them together into a large drawing that represented about half of the pyramid. It was like doing a jigsaw puzzle, because I wanted the detailed areas to be interesting, not only in themselves, but also in how they related to the detailed areas around them." Meanwhile the model shop launched into the basic shape.

"First we built a foam-core mockup," said Mark Stetson, "and that was used as a study model so that the form could be evaluated for camera angles. Foam-core board is a composite structural material that's used a lot in motion picture work for building big, lightweight flats. Basically, it's paperboard with a styrofoam center — about a quarter-inch thick — and it comes in four-by-eight sheets. So it's more structural than cardboard. The pyramid, in fact, was particularly strong because the pyramidal shape is actually a very high-strength form. In the end, that mockup really saved us a lot, because Doug had originally envisioned the pyramid as a sixteen-foot model so he could get enough depth of field on it. The mockup we did was only eight feet, but when he saw the still photographs of the approach to our half-scale pyramid, he said: 'That's fine. That's enough.' And that really saved us a lot of time. The detail we applied to

Model shop crew members Chris Ross, Michael McMillen and Wayne Smith reposition a preliminary foam-core representation of the Tyrell pyramid. Intended originally as a half-scale mockup, the eight-foot structure was to prove doubly useful when subsequent photographic tests indicated that it was already large enough to hold sufficient depth of field. As a result, the final pyramid could be made to the same scale. / Working from dozens of thumbnail sketches, designer Tom Cranham prepares a detailed drawing of the pyramid's terraced face. / Extrapolating from Cranham's basic design, modelmaker Bill George details a master mold pattern which will later be replicated in clear casting resin and symmetrically repeated around the monolithic structure. / John Vidor scrapes paint away from designated window areas so the model can be lit simply from within. / Crouched inside the pyramid, Kris Gregg adds finishing touches to the highly-detailed miniature.

CINEFEX 9 ► 15

The buttresses were constructed over hollow lightboxes and detailed by Chris Ross, who covered the illuminated outer surfaces — first with random window patterns on high-contrast film, and then with two separate layers of intricate acid-etched brass. / Once completed, the buttresses were positioned in pairs around the base of the pyramid. / The finished structure was then transported to the EEG shooting stages where it was carefully lit and photographed with a large-format still camera to produce the front projection plates required for the first day's shooting.

that pyramid was very delicate and fine; and frankly, I can't imagine doing one twice that size."

Once the overall size was diminished, it became theoretically possible to complete the project before principal photography began. "Lighting the model was always a major concern," Stetson continued. "It was supposed to be a city unto itself, with thousands upon thousands of light sources. And we knew that if we tried to fiber optic it, we'd have to live with round light sources — and we'd have to live with an awful lot of work. So to save that fiber optic step in the pyramid body, I thought about going to a clear casting technique. We experimented with various urethanes and stuff, and found that clear polyester resin was perfectly adequate and a lot cheaper. It was always our plan to use a mold-making technique, which allows you to put a lot of effort into a master or a series of masters and then have them repeated endlessly. Since the pyramid required pretty accurate geometry, our foam-core mockup came in very handy as a guide. We cut acrylic template patterns to fit the mockup accurately, and then we worked on them for our rubber mold patterns — detailing them with strips of styrene and limited model kit parts. Bill George did most of that. Then we made our rubber molds. Since there's always a natural shrinkage in rubber molds, we were concerned about the geometry holding up in the resultant castings. As a result, we decided to try cutting acrylic panels to the original pattern sizes of all the pieces we had used to assemble the original pyramid shape. The molds we prepared by spraying them first with a primer coat and then with an opaquing fluid. After that we'd pour in clear casting resin and then push the precut acrylic pieces into place, which stretched the rubber molds back to their original size. When the polyester cured, it cured right to the acrylic, and those sandwiched shapes then became our structural pieces — which were transparent except for the outer skin that we'd opaqued in the molds.

"After the parts were cast and preliminary assembly began, we put a 2K light source behind the partially built pyramid, and John Vidor — in a pair of headphones and a Sony Walkman — did nothing but scrape windows for a week. We'd made little chisel-like cutting tools out of X-acto knives, and by using those he was able to scrape the opaque paint away and make these little sixteenth-inch square windows. Even though it was an angled pyramid face, it was a terraced pyramid and there were areas that were obviously assigned to windows. So it was pretty easy to scrape, but it had to be done in a random pattern so that it looked like there were lights in some windows, and in other windows there weren't. The buttresses we did in a different way. They were basically hollow lightboxes with layered artwork to convey a sense of structure and to break up the light into recognizably architectural patterns. Chris Ross did almost all of that. First he would lay down a piece of high-contrast film with a random window pattern on it. Over that he laid a regular grid of rectangularly-etched brass sheet; and then over that was yet another grid of brass that was a little more decorative — not quite as regular and rigid. All together, the effect looked like you're looking through the facade of a massive piece of architecture, behind which was a framework that broke up the windows, behind which was the high-contrast film that suggested that some of the windows were lit and some were not. And once again, we were able to get an awful lot out of a limited investment in masters. The result of all this was that with four or five small fluorescent bulbs per buttress, plus a bare-bulb 5K lamp inside the basic structure, we had the whole pyramid lit. And then, for detail, we went back with our pretty much state-of-the-art axial lights and a few fiber optics here and there, just to add a little interest to it."

The overall buttress structures did, however, generate some early concern among the model builders. "When I first put them in," Tom Cranham explained, "Mark and some of the guys in the model shop thought that we ought to put columns in to support them from the back. They felt that having those kinds of structures at such angles would cause gravity to pull them down. But my feeling was that, at this point in the future, they would have materials designed to withstand such stresses. Already there are laminated materials much like a honeycomb — very lightweight, but with much greater strength than steel and perhaps about one-tenth the weight. So to me, it was conceivable that these structures of the future could exist at those angles and still withstand gravity without any problem. Ultimately, the supports *were* left out; and I'm glad, because I think they would have destroyed some of the geometry of the building."

The final miniature — including the buttresses — was nine feet square at the base, two-and-a-half feet tall, and represented only the top two-thirds of Cranham's original design. The full pyramid shape would be featured only in longer shots, and for those a graduated series of much smaller miniatures was planned. When Douglas Trumbull saw the completed upper portion, however, he decided it was perfectly adequate by itself, and so the bottom third was simply deleted from the overall concept. And since the approved storyboards involved only unidirectorial flybys of the massive pyramids, the model shop found it necessary to build only a two-sided structure. "We concentrated, of course, on those areas that had been storyboarded for close flyovers and whatnot," said Stetson, "and we made up a lot of patterns for those areas. So where it was important, we had vast expanses with no apparent seams — except on corners and major detail lines where they belonged. Then, for the less important areas — areas behind the buttresses and on the lower parts of the pyramid — we chopped up patterns that we had already made and just reassembled them like a jigsaw puzzle."

Working at breakneck pace, the model crew finished the basic pyramid a week before their already accelerated deadline, just barely in time for it to be photographed in large format by still photographer Virgil Mirano, enhanced by airbrush artist Cy Didjurgis, and readied in time for the main unit's first day of shooting in the Tyrell office set. Coordinating always with director of photography Jordan Cronenweth, Douglas Trumbull and Richard Yuricich carefully aligned one of their 65mm matte

CINEFEX 9 ▶ 17

18 ◀ CINEFEX 9

cameras to the 8x10 plate projector which had last seen extensive use on *Close Encounters*, and front-projected the just-completed pyramid into the expansive window area of Lawrence Paull's imposing set, creating a dramatic backdrop for Deckard's visit to the corporation headquarters and his first dissettling encounter with the enigmatic Rachael. Matthew Yuricich, who had already put three weeks in on the unused backup painting, was by no means off the hook, however.

"The first three days were spent shooting in the Tyrell office," said Richard Yuricich. "We broke a cardinal rule in front projection and backlit the whole set. That causes *lots* of problems, because the nearer to the axis of projection you get a lamp — whether it's going away or coming towards you — the more likely you are to have problems with flare. But that was the look Ridley was after; and with Douglas around, there's no such thing as a rule that can't be broken. So we backlit the whole set as though the sun were just above the horizon, and placed the lights carefully in such a way that we had a maximum backlight effect with a minimum of flare in the beam splitter. Then we had to go back in and do a matte painting for the upper portion of the frame — both to put in clouds and things, but more so to hide the arcs that we'd put above and behind the screen to light the set."

The painting assignment, naturally enough, fell to Matthew Yuricich. "The way the shot was set up, the front projection screen didn't reach all the way to the top of the frame. Instead, it cut right through the sky area. Well, it's very difficult to match a painting through sky, and Ridley wanted some clouds anyway. So I ended up painting out everything that I could — right down to the tops of their heads." In addition to those areas of the frame that were strictly matte painting, Yuricich also enhanced portions of the live-action. Because the set lighting was predominantly from the rear, some of the foreground columns ended up being darker than desired. To remedy the situation, Yuricich painted just the slightest suggestion of the underexposed areas onto his matte board. Since the enhanced areas were below the designated matte line, when the overall painting was photographed, those areas were thus superimposed over the previously under-defined live-action to provide supplemental highlights and detail. It was a technique Yuricich was to employ on several other *Blade Runner* paintings as well.

After the fact, it was decided that since the office scenes were so heavily backlit, there should probably also be a visible sun. Animation supervisor John Wash was assigned to the task. Another USC cinema graduate, Wash had had previous feature film experience on *Dark Star*, and had worked on graphics and computer animation for *Star Wars* — but his strongest mark had been made in the area of independent industrial films, TV station logos and commercial effects. His demo reel and a recommendation from both David Dryer and Nick Vasu — an old friend and associate of Richard Yuricich — secured for him a billet on the *Blade Runner* team. Working closely with him was animation cameraman Glenn Campbell, a seasoned veteran of *Star Trek – The Motion Picture*, and a variety of subsequent projects at the Universal Hartland effects facility.

"That sun was John Wash's pride and joy," Campbell commented. "He spent a great deal of time wedging and timing it so it would drop right in perfectly. It was a two-element shot. The first pass was to get just the glow around the sun that lit up the general vicinity of the sky around the building. It was done with backlit art and the sun was about the size of a quarter. On top of that we had to put a holdout matte for the edge of the building — which was difficult to do because I had to rotoscope it off of a murky front projection plate of the buildings lost in the haze, and it was tough to get any straight lines. Then, on top of that, we put about a quarter-inch opal — which is kind of a milky white plastic sheet that just diffuses light like you wouldn't believe. Then finally, we put a black dot over the opal to matte out the actual sun area itself, which we put in on the second pass. So what we got in the end was this sort of off-white, orange-yellow sun, with a tremendous orange-red glow around it that bled off into the sky. It looked very, very natural."

The most complicating aspect of the shot was that Sean Young — playing Rachael — crosses during the scene and walks directly in front of the sun. To preclude the sun's being burned in over her as well as the exterior background, assistant cameraman Alan Harding produced an articulate rotoscope matte. "It was only about eighteen frames," said Campbell, "but it was still pretty interesting, because we wanted to make sure that she didn't look like a cutout. So Alan went through and roto'd her exactly; and then we chopped down her matte, so that when she walks in front of the sun it actually bleeds around her. The matte was just smaller than her body, so it wiped out her edges before she actually started holding it out — exactly as it would if you were photographing it live on a set."

As further enhancements to the shot, tiny points of light representing distant spinners were also incorporated, and at one point early in the sequence a larger spinner was even matted in on a landing approach. "It worked technically," revealed David Dryer, who supervised the postproduction enhancement phase, "but like so many other things in effect, you have to then say: 'Wait a minute. Do we really want this?' Because that was to be Rachael's first appearance in the film and ultimately we felt it detracted from her entrance. So even though it worked, we dropped it." As the sequence progresses, a photosensitive blind is lowered over the window to darken the outside. Like most of the other elements in the shot, that too was added during the postproduction phase — using a neutral density filter material to partially obscure the light.

"One interesting thing about the sun," Glenn Campbell concluded, "is that it moves during the course of the scene. When you first see it, it's just intersecting the edge of the building. But during the sequence, we cut back every so often and you'll notice the sun is rising up in the frame. In the last shot, as the blinds come down — which Don Baker animated with holdouts for the columns that were generated on the matte stand — the sun is not visible at all. We simply shot the glow at the very top of

Deckard's initial encounter with Rachael transpires inside the pyramid — in Tyrell's executive suite which featured a massive expanse of glass and an early morning view of a second pyramid nearby. In reality, the imposing set was open in the back, with a large Scotchlite screen positioned in such a way that the window imagery could be carefully aligned and front-projected in during principal photography. Since the set extended above the screen, matte artist Matthew Yuricich was called upon to paint in the upper portion of the frame. / On the EEG custom matte stand, camera assistant Tama Takahashi scrapes white paint away from the background matte glass, while matte cameraman Robert Bailey paints a soft-edged matte on a foreground glass to help blend the live-action and painted images. / After painting and live-action were combined, animation supervisor John Wash added a glowing sun using backlit animation techniques.

Douglas Trumbull discusses a scene with his director of miniature photography, Dave Stewart. / For a sequence in which Deckard uses a computerized Esper terminal to study a holographic snapshot, EEG was tasked with providing appropriate footage to be filmed off a video monitor during the live-action shoot. The effect of moving through the three-dimensional still image was created by taking a progressive series of still photographs — with five-second time exposures so actor Rutger Hauer could move his head toward the camera, as though caught unaware by a candid shutterbug. These stills were then linked together on an animation stand by cameraman Don Baker, who used a flash-and-fade technique and superimposed graphic readouts as his subjective camera appeared to prowl through the room.

the frame."

Although the Tyrell pyramid was the most pressing preproduction requirement, other aspects of the film also demanded consideration. The opening sequence, for example, involved a confrontation between Deckard's friend, Holden, and the replicant Leon. In order to clearly determine that Leon is nonhuman, Holden administers the Voight-Kampff test which measures empathic response — a strictly human characteristic the replicants cannot successfully simulate. "The Voight-Kampff machine is sort of like an exotic lie detector," explained Syd Mead, "that zeroes in on your eye and measures iris contraction and sniffs the air — because when you're nervous you perspire and give off an odor trace. So the machine sucks in air from around the person being interviewed, and then runs it through an analyzer. And so we had to come up with a device that was briefcase size, but had a very ominous look to it. One of the things I liked most about Ridley was that he could coach you along by giving you almost tactile word pictures of what he was after. And in this case he said: 'I want this thing to sit on the desk and have the same frightening, but delicate, kind of look that a big spider would have if it suddenly crawled out of a desk drawer and was sitting there on your ink blotter.' And he drew a little sketch. One of the things it needed was a little video screen; and fortunately, Sony had just come out with about a one-and-a-half-inch diagonal color screen for the eyepiece monitor in their cameras. And so we used those, and finally came up with this delicate machine that unfolds itself and has little bellows and goes up and down and looks very, very intricate. And it also looks very ominous because it's motorized and this little arm with a small triangular lens on the end would lift up and sort of move around and lock in on you."

Jamie Shourt, whose most recent film assignment had been the construction of *Heartbeeps'* fully mechanized robot, Phil, was commissioned to build the articulated Voight-Kampff machine. Shortly before it was actually required, it was delivered to the production company. "From what I heard," said Bill George, "when the first Voight-Kampff was demonstrated to Ridley, it fell apart in front of him. Around that time, we had finished the pyramid. Everybody liked it, so they gave us the old Voight-Kampff pieces and a three-day deadline to build a new one. The project went real well considering we all worked on separate sections that eventually had to come together. It was like each person was building a single piece of a jigsaw puzzle."

"During the course of the interview," said David Dryer, "even though the dialogue doesn't indicate anything, it's clear that Holden and Leon are antagonists. The scene starts in wide shots and then gets tighter and tighter as the drama builds, until finally all you see are these two guys reflected in each other's eyeballs. Of course, most of the sequence was shot in 35mm, but the eyeball shots were done in 65mm — which was a problem, because there's not a lens in 65mm that will give you that shot. So what we had to do was create a bellows extension, which ended up being almost four feet long — with an effective loss of over four stops in exposure. Of course, we were limited in how much light we could pour into somebody's eye without damaging it; and Ridley wanted the irises to move, which made it even more difficult. For the reflected images, we took a 9.8mm fisheye lens — a still lens actually — and put it on our 65mm camera and shot the actors with the desk and the primary props against black. The image we got back was circular, and then we made partial holdout mattes — so there'd still be some transparency — and composited them with the eyeball footage. The eyeball footage had been taken with the original actors, and even though they did their best to remain still, even the slightest movement created major problems for the lineup guys in optical. In fact, Dick Rippel — who was responsible for the shots — was having such an awful time trying to track them that he finally said: 'Okay. Let's do it over. And this time we're going to use *my* eye, because I'm the guy who really knows how important it is to be still.' Fortunately, his eyes were almost identical in color to both of the actors, so it worked out fine."

When Leon senses impending failure of the empathy test, he responds by suddenly drawing a concealed blaster and firing at Holden. "Ridley wanted to have an unusual, futuristic gun," said Douglas Trumbull, "either a laser gun or a particle beam weapon or something. With these kinds of things, the trend has been to have a flash of light and a lot of smoke and a laser beam or something that's rotoscoped into the shot, like on *Star Wars.* But one of the things I always try to do — I think maybe I learned this from Stanley Kubrick — is whatever you think of first, try to do the opposite. So I said: 'Why not make something that's black? Instead of making light come out of the gun, make darkness come out. And rather than make things explode, have them *implode* — collapse — as though matter just vaporized and vanished into a void.' It wouldn't throw blood and gore all over the place — part of him would just vanish. And I proposed some ways to do shockwaves on the set. One of them, in fact, was based on the same principal as a toy space-gun that's been around for years. Essentially, there's a rubber diaphragm inside and when you cock the weapon the diaphragm sort of pulls back like a speaker cone. Then there's a venturi cone on the front, and as soon as you let the thing go, it makes an instantaneous pulse of air that can travel as a ball right across the room. So one of the things I wanted to do was build a huge one of these that you could direct at an actor or a set or anything. It wouldn't be enough to blow things away, but everything would kind of react to it for an instant. Then there'd have to be some dummies made that could implode, so that clothing and things would be sucked into a hole. The black beam, or black area, we could do as an optical effect. But somehow, in spite of Ridley liking the idea and us liking the idea, the physical effects crew on the picture did not respond as needed. In fact, I think the original physical effects people on the picture misestimated just about everything. They were not delivering props and effects solutions on time, and one week prior to principal photography they were fired and replaced. As a result, though, unfortunately a lot of ideas just sort of fell between the cracks. So when it came time to actually shoot the scene, they had rigged it with all kinds of pyrotechnic flashes and wire gags, and it was just the same old thing all over."

Another short-notice requirement called for the production of a one-minute film sequence to be transferred to video and used in Deckard's home Esper terminal as he studies a small snapshot he had found in Leon's hotel room. "I suggested that they use a little card of plastic that looks sort of like a video disc," said Trumbull, "with some sort of holographic image imbedded in there that you can't really see without putting it in a viewer. Deckard takes it and sticks it in this sort of video monitor thing; and he's able to just verbally tell the device to turn left, turn right, enlarge, enhance, process, or whatever, this image. We did the footage for that using still photographs, and we set up this little set on the stage off to the side of Tyrell's office. The photo Deckard was studying was supposed to be a guy sitting at a desk in this kind of old-style apartment, and we did enormously careful lighting to give it almost a Rembrandt painting-type look. There was the guy and the desk, and on the desk was a lamp that threw this pool of light that was very warm and kind of sepia-tone; and then the rest of the room was sort of dark, with all this old furniture around. It was very atmospheric. Then, way off in the next room, about twenty feet away, was a mirror on the wall that reflected the other side of the room that you couldn't actually see. And in that reflection was a boudoir which had mirrors on the doors reflecting the image of someone on a bed which was even *farther* out of the picture. After we lit this whole thing very carefully, we brought in Rutger Hauer — who was supposed to be sitting at the desk — and shot this whole series of rather strange photographs. For one thing, we wanted to make it look like kind of a candid snapshot; and at the moment the picture was taken, the guy's just turning toward the camera, so his face is blurred. To do that, we came up with a little beeper — like a metronome beeper — that would go off when the camera shutter opened. That would be Rutger's cue to start turning his head; and there'd be about a five-second exposure. Then we set up a motorized Nikon with the right lens and the right exposure, and put the camera on a dolly so we could shoot from a whole series of different positions and actually physically move through the room, panning and tilting in sequence, with each photograph being about a foot away from the other. For the areas that were going to be scrutinized in more detail, we also shot a number of large-format, eight-by-ten transparencies. So what we had was this whole series of photographs, and on each of them Rutger was blurred the same way. We ended up going right in close on his face, which is blurred now a foot horizontally as he turns his head. It's not even recognizable. Then the camera moves down to the table and looks at the props there, and then zooms back to his face, and looks over his shoulder and sees this mirror on a table in the next room, and then moves in there. And there's this whole tableau of an old wine bottle and a clock and a mirror and a couple other things on this table top, and it all looks sort of like a Rembrandt-lit still-life. The camera zooms in on the reflection

22 ◀ CINEFEX 9

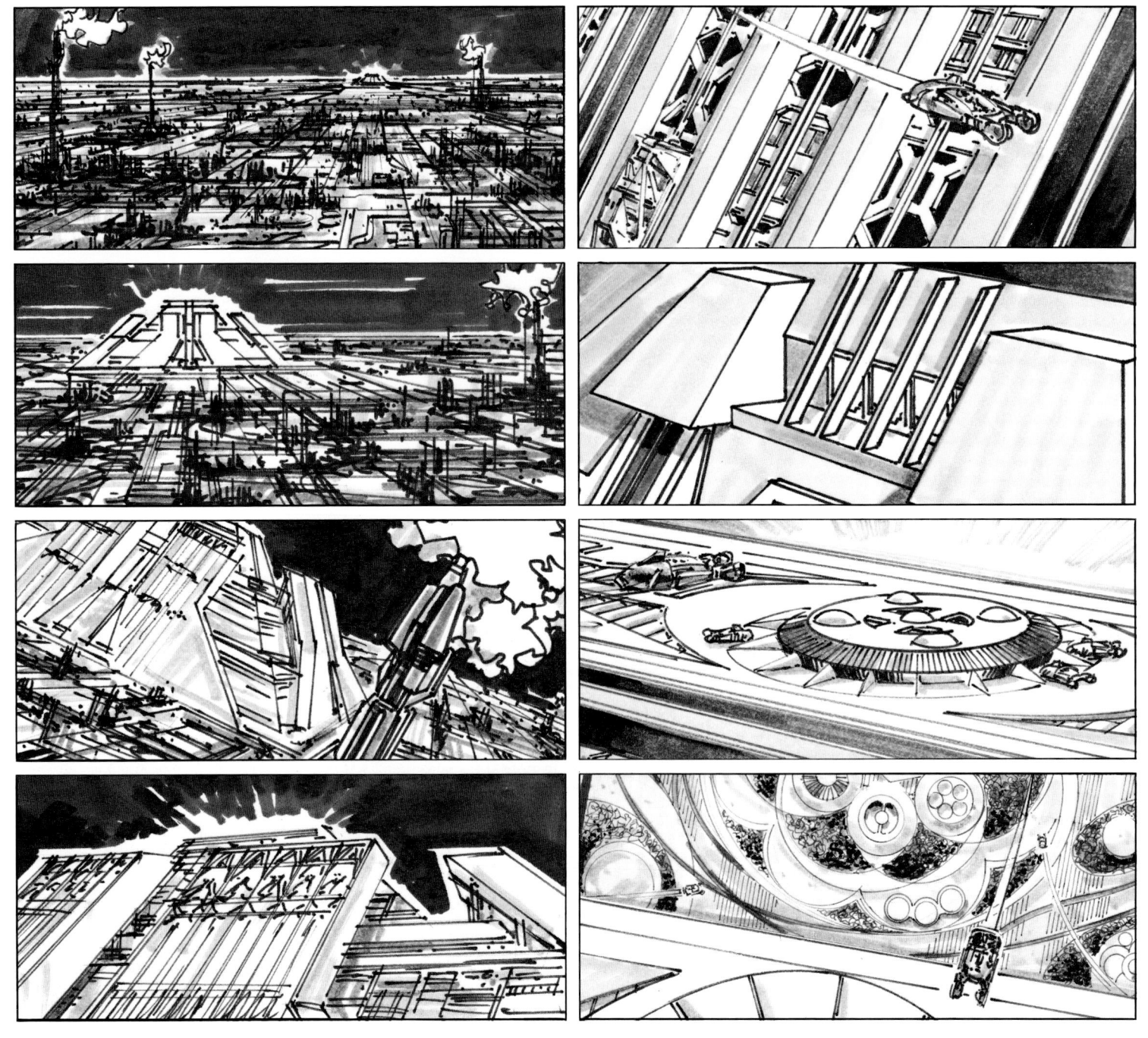

in the mirror and then proceeds to reverse and go across the room to the boudoir, which is open, and all the way up to microphotography of the sequins on a dress — one of which provides a clue because it's some kind of silica-type disc. Then it moves over to the mirror on the boudoir to see this woman lying on the bed. It goes into the reflection, and we shot a bunch of flopped stills of the woman in bed and zoomed in on a tattoo on her arm.

"After all that was done, Don Baker shot this whole sequence on an animation stand using sort of a flash-and-fade technique. About every six frames you'd see one of these stills, and it would go flash and then fade; and the next one would come up and it'd go flash and fade; and each one was a little closer — a little more magnified version. It looked really neat. Then all that was transferred to videotape and displayed on a monitor while Deckard's sitting there giving verbal commands: 'Turn left . . . turn right . . . move in . . . process . . . enhance . . .' It was a weird, kind of voyeuristic scene, as though that one holographic image had everything in the whole building recorded on one little frame." Due to a last-minute change in the live-action shooting schedule, Don Baker ultimately found himself with only a three-day deadline to produce the required Esper footage, which involved not only rephotographing the stills on motion picture film, but also designing and preparing numerous graphics elements as well. Once everything was ready to shoot, he rented time on a 35mm animation stand at Nick Vasu, Inc., in Hollywood, spent forty-eight straight hours on the job, slept a bit in the lab parking lot while it was being processed, and then took it immediately to be transferred onto videotape.

Once the initial front projection plate requirements were out of the way, the pyramid was turned over to Dave Stewart's stage crew, which included cameraman David Hardberger and "model wranglers" Bob Spurlock and Pat Van Auken, who had hands-on responsibility for working with the miniatures on-stage. After the basic setup was established, members of the model shop crew were called in to add further last-minute embellishments and make subtle alterations in the glistening paint job. Meanwhile, for even closer shots, another miniature was already in the works. "We built an enlarged-scale insert model for the peak of the main pyramidal shape where Tyrell's office was meant to be," Mark Stetson revealed. "The whole model was about five feet wide by four feet tall, but the little office area itself was only about six inches square. Nevertheless, Leslie Ekker built a beautifully detailed little interior, from plans provided by the art department, that matched the full-size set perfectly. He also built some little one-inch-long spinner models to land on the pads and lit some of them with axial lights. We also built a little rear projection screen into the model to represent the lower office where Holden interrogates Leon. The idea was that the camera would move right in on that and you'd actually be able to see inside the full-size set. The insert model also featured the exterior elevators — three of which were wired in to motion control cable-drive mechanisms — the plateau landing areas, and the very top of the pyramid before you enter the well of darkness."

The well of darkness, a huge gaping abyss leading nowhere, was actually an unused leftover from an earlier concept which had the pyramid structurally resembling a volcano. "The original pyramid was hollowed out," revealed Tom Cranham, who storyboarded the opening flight to the Tyrell complex, "and inside the hollow core there was a whole different world of clean air and green parks and things of that sort. But I guess it wasn't a strong enough story point to carry it out in terms of the problems it presented and the expense."

Like most of the miniatures used in *Blade Runner*, the pyramid was destined to be shot in a smoke environment, both to suggest the polluted atmosphere that permeates the film, but also to impart a sense of great mass and appropriate aerial perspective. The technique, which Trumbull and his effects unit had pioneered on *Close Encounters of the Third Kind* to create an armada of luminous UFOs, and which had been used to somewhat different effect in *Star Trek*'s V'ger photography, required primarily a sealed stage into which a diffusing medium of some sort could be pumped. As in many effects facilities, the EEG stage area is devoid of hard walls, thus allowing maximum flexibility in configuring the space to suit the particular demands of a given project. As needed, individual stages are created by hanging heavy black curtains which serve both to block unwanted light from neighboring stage and nonstage areas and also to absorb troublesome reflections from the inside. Though fabric is generally used for routine photography, a dense nonporous plastic material was employed for the smoke room walls. "Halfway through the production," said Dave Stewart, "the fire department came in on inspection and told us we shouldn't be using it because it's very flammable. Fortunately, they agreed to let us finish the movie with it, but next time it'll have to be replaced with rubber — which I think is probably pretty appropriate. I've always said that special effects needs a rubber room."

In actuality, the Mole-Richardson bee smoke used in the smoke room is not smoke at all, but rather a low-grade diesel fuel which is vaporized — not burned — to produce a fine mist of suspended oil in the air. Though breathable, it does not provide an ideal environment for long-term human exposure, and so most of the crew members working inside the smoke room wear filtering gas masks. Outside the room, the liquid smoke base is electrically heated until it vaporizes, and then it is picked up by fans and blown into the stage area. A battery of fans inside keep the vapor moving so it does not settle in clouds. Then, since most of the shots require very long exposures — sometimes running into hours — an optical smoke-sensing system is employed to monitor and regulate the smoke density. Infrared light beams are directed across the stage to receiver units; and if the density is getting low, the smoke machine is triggered to automatically pump more smoke into the room.

Since the pyramid was the first miniature to be completed, and since the basic close-in photography of it would later need to be augmented with various traveling matte and animation elements,

A series of images extracted from Tom Cranham's original storyboard for the opening Hades flyover and approach to the Tyrell headquarters. Though essentially unchanged, the sequence was originally to have featured only a single pyramid, and the final overpass was to have revealed a hollow central core replete with clean air and landscaped greenery.

Final pyramid assembly and last-minute detailing were effected in the EEG smoke room. Since all camera angles were generally unidirectional, a two-sided pyramid was deemed sufficient, and only those surfaces exposed to view were fully finished. Separate in-camera passes were necessary for proper balance of external and internal light sources, with the two-pyramid tracking shots requiring separate film elements as well — carefully timed and aligned to permit later compositing in optical. / Douglas Trumbull inspects the almost-completed pyramid. / Cameraman David Hardberger previews a motion control move. Once the move is recorded and approved, the system runs virtually unattended during actual photography. Lengthy exposures, dictated by low-level lighting and the need for total depth of field, resulted in many shots taking hours or days before all the various production and matte passes could be completed.

it was also the first thing to go before the cameras. Most of the shots involved fluid camera movement — along with multiple in-camera passes to build up an image of the pyramid and insure that all of its many practical light sources were properly exposed with relation to one another. Though some updated motion control units had been rented from Universal after the studio shuttered its Hartland effects facility, Dave Stewart used the original system designed and constructed by Jerry Jeffress for *Close Encounters*. Dubbed the "Icebox" because of its squarish upright shape, the prototype device was still current and useful, and was capable of recording and controlling up to eight channels of movement. The hulking 65mm cameras preferred by Trumbull and his associates were mounted on tracks, and through use of a joystick mechanism linked to the motion controller, the cameramen were able to "fly" the camera — running it up and down the track, panning and tilting. By programming and recording one axis of movement at a time, the operator was thus able to build up a smooth composite move that could later be played back repeatedly and accurately.

Precise repeatability is critical to EEG's way of doing business, even more than it is for Industrial Light and Magic or Apogee or any of the other effect houses that utilize bluescreen traveling mattes as their primary compositing tool. For unlike the bluescreen process, where the all-important mattes are extracted from the original production photography, the Trumbull technique is a pure offspring of motion control technology. Miniatures, for the most part, are photographed first against black backgrounds, with as many in-camera passes as necessary to build the desired image. The matte is then produced on a separate pass entirely. In the case of the pyramid, a frontlit-backlit technique — used throughout most of *Close Encounters* and much of *Star Trek* — was employed. The frontlit pass is used for the basic model photography; then a backlit pass is used to generate the matte. On the frontlit pass, the model is photographed against black. But for the backlit pass, a white card or screen is placed behind the miniature so that — from the camera's point of view — the miniature is always surrounded by white. During the matte pass, the white backdrop is lit uniformly, while the model itself is left totally unilluminated. The resultant image is a black silhouette of the miniature against a white background; and from this piece of photography, the EEG optical department can generate whatever holdout or cover mattes may be required for compositing. Even though the desired end result is a black-and-white matte, the same color negative film stock used for the frontlit pass is used for the backlit one. "The mattes can be generated from the color negative with no problem," explained Dave Stewart. "What's important is that you have the same grain structure as the original, the same amount of reflectance to light, the same blur characteristics, and the same thickness of film. That's why we use the same film stock. If you have all that, your chances of a perfect fit are much better."

Since only one pyramid was actually constructed, the two-pyramid shots required Stewart and his crew to produce separate, identically-timed, but offset camera passes on the single miniature — with corresponding mattes — so the two images could be overlapped and sandwiched together later in optical. And though generally it was not the case, for one static shot in which the pyramids are shown standing side-by-side, the two images were shot in sequence on an in-camera composite and then tied together later with a Matthew Yuricich matte painting.

The final approach shot required an emergency call to the model shop. "The camera was supposed to take you from outside the pyramid right into the small office," said Bill George. "A process plate was shot out on the lot, and it was supposed to be rear-projected into the large pyramid section. Later, however, it was discovered that the angle of the process plate did not match the required angle of approach. After a few tries with rear projection, it was decided instead to build a miniature office into the pyramid section. The problem was that it was only about an inch-and-a-half square, and no matter how detailed a miniature is, at that size it just never looks real — especially when it fills a quarter of the screen. What saved it was the fact that on the full-size set, there were large rotating fans just above the desks. Because of the angle of approach, you could barely see the fans, but they were in there — under motion control — and there were tiny lensed bulbs near the ceiling that projected their moving shadows on the back wall. And that subtle movement in the miniature set gave it a much greater feeling of realism."

Though closeup photography on the pyramid consumed several exacting weeks of stage time, the Tyrell corporate headquarters did not exist in a vacuum — and before anything further could be accomplished, its surrounding environment had to be realized. Appropriately enough, the vast refinery-like complex, belching flame and noxious pollutants into the neighboring skies, became known as the Hades landscape. "One of the early ideas that I had," said Tom Cranham, "was to make this massive Hades area surrounding the pyramids all murky and smoke-filled and rust-colored, and just the epitome of the worst smog day you can imagine multiplied a hundredfold. And then there'd be an inversion layer over this, so that as you approached the pyramids you'd fly up through the inversion layer and break out into the clear, and you'd see the tops of these two pyramids glistening like jewels above this murky layer below." Whether because of technical problems, or because such a concept would have obstructed a clear master shot of the Tyrell pyramids, Cranham's concept was ultimately vetoed and the decision was made to maintain a consistently smog-laden environment throughout. The solution as to how to achieve it pictorially came from Douglas Trumbull. "Once Ridley decided that he want this sort of infinite industrial landscape kind of thing, I came up with the idea of using — for the most part, anyway — a series of forced-perspective cutouts of towers and cables and things that we could produce in quantity with this etched brass technique we discovered that would really give us *tremendous* detail. The etched brass pieces would be arranged on big plexiglass sheets so the whole thing could be lit from below, and there'd be fiber

CINEFEX 9 ► 25

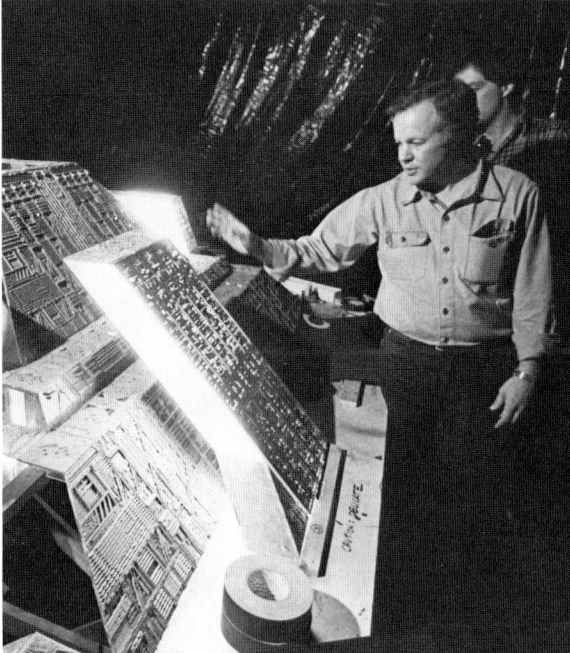

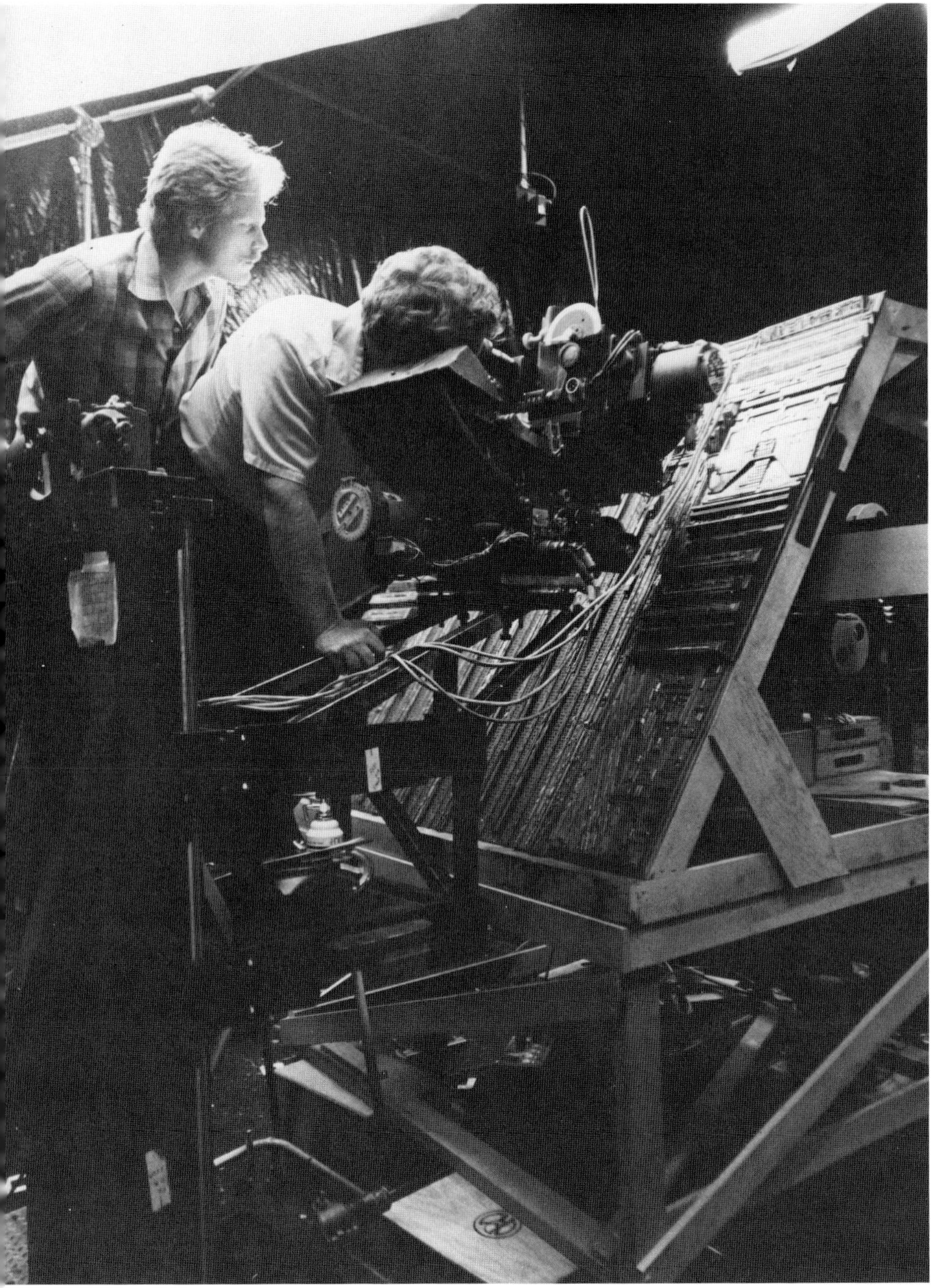

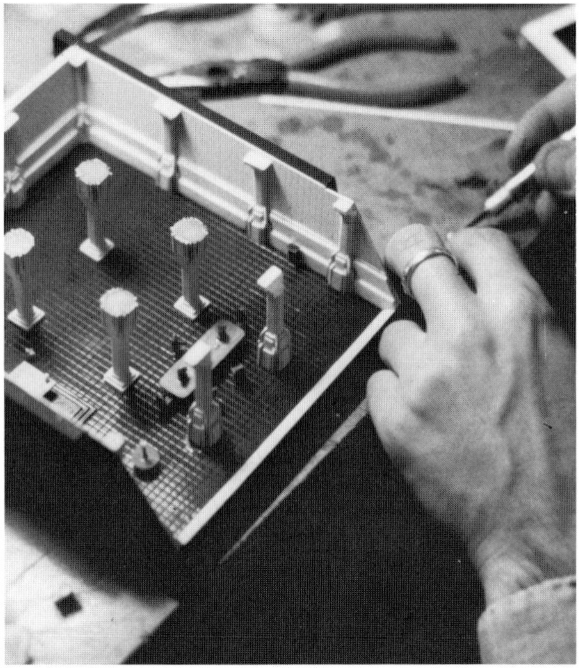

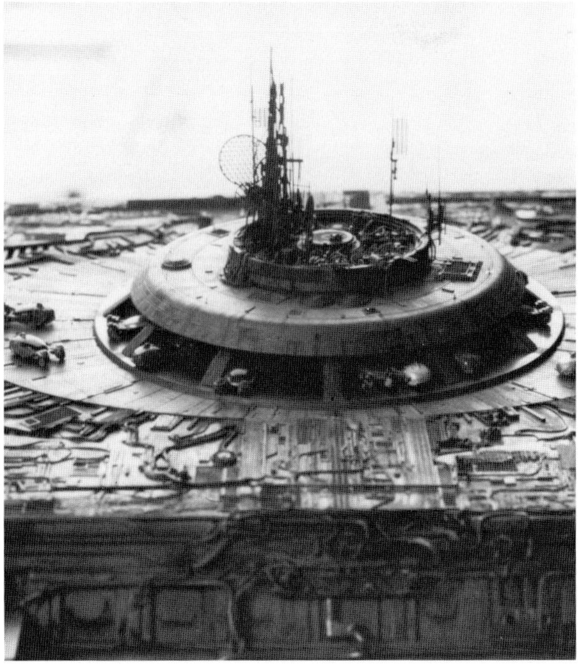

optics built in everywhere. Then, to really top it off, there'd be explosions and flames coming out of some of the stacks. It was a pretty exciting concept, and it took a lot of time to get it executed — but it worked great."

Since the etched brass technique required, as a basis, some sort of black-and-white artwork or graphics, it was decided that a good way to begin the project would be to photograph some actual oil refineries and use those reality-based images as a starting point for extrapolation and enhancement. With that in mind, Mark Stetson and still photographer Virgil Mirano drove down to El Segundo and spent a day wandering around the expansive oil refineries in the area. "We took a great many shots," said Mirano, "using high-contrast black-and-white film in order to drop away the gray areas, and framing all these cracking towers and other structures against the sky so we could get silhouettes. Then I took those and made large sixteen-by-twenty black-and-white prints, again attempting to drop away as much of the intermediate tones as possible. Those prints were then assembled and reassembled, photographed again in the vertical process camera, and then made into hi-con prints." At that point, they were turned over to modelmaker Chris Ross, who was going to make his own pen-and-ink refinements and modifications.

"Our original thinking was that it would be easier to dress up some real stuff than it would be to actually create the artwork," said Mark Stetson, "but Chris soon found that it was a lot easier for him just to draw from scratch. He wouldn't be tied to anything but his imagination, and he could get more bizarre shapes that way." Once the artwork was completed, in a variety of sizes and scales, high-contrast film negatives were made and then turned over to a commercial firm in El Segundo that specialized in acid etching. The process involves coating the metal or plastic substrate — in this case brass, because it was easily solderable — with a photo-resist material. The high-contrast film negatives are then contact-exposed onto the brass sheet, and the emulsion is processed, leaving the exposed photo-resist behind, but washing the rest away. Next, it is sent through a conveyor with a sulfuric acid spray. The photo-resist image areas are unaffected by the acid, but the unprotected areas are gradually eaten away, leaving a thin, remarkably intricate, but sturdy brass silhouette of the original artwork.

"Doug had originally said that he wanted the Hades landscape to be fifteen or eighteen feet wide," said Stetson, "and so we made it eighteen feet wide and thirteen feet deep. The first step was to build the table, which was about two-thirds plexiglass so we could shine lights up from below. We had it set up originally as a forced-perspective model, but realized soon that Ridley and Doug didn't want to be tied to a single point of view. So we then changed it over to more of a diminishing perspective — the difference being that the forced perspective model could be shot from only one point of view, whereas the diminishing perspective one would be suitable from a general camera angle. That meant it had to be pretty random. There couldn't be too much on it that would indicate an organization and give away the scale change. As a result, we couldn't radiate our etched brass pieces out from camera — which would have made it a little more effective, but it would have cut down on our versatility. Instead, we laid them out in rows, but staggered and randomly, so there wasn't a straight row that ran all the way across the model. The sizes ranged from about a half-an-inch high in the back to eight inches high in the front, and we just hot-glued them to the plexiglass. But as we got into putting the thing together, we realized quickly that the etched metal stuff would have given away the trick if we'd used it too close to the foreground. So we backed up and started making foam patterns for foreground structures — just urethane foam cast into rubber molds. Foam is very fast and it's easy to poke fiber optics through; and we just built up a whole bunch of towers and things from the larger etched metal pieces and a lot of plastic model kit parts. So in the end, the entire front third of the model was cast-foam based. In addition, Chris Ross also built three 'hero' towers. Those had the very best detail and they were separate from the model board itself. That way they could be mounted individually on C-stands and positioned in front of the actual model so the camera could fly right by them."

Unlike the pyramid, the Hades landscape offered no quick-and-easy solution to the problem of practical lighting. "With the pyramid we were fortunate in that we had an architectural form that allowed us to do our little window scrape trick and get away with a single light source inside. With the Hades landscape, we had to go to fiber optics. In fact, we hadn't really given a whole lot of thought to lighting it at all until one evening when I happened to be flying out of L.A. on a trip up to San Francisco, and I looked out and *all* I could see was lights. I got back and ordered seven miles of fiber optics. Holes were drilled in the plexiglass base of the model and the fiber optics were threaded up from beneath the table and positioned behind the etched-metal grids, with just the tip of the fiber optic facing the camera. The light sources were made up very quickly — just little wooden boxes with fans and bulbs and metal conduit to bundle the fibers. There were about thirty of those. Then, along with the miles and miles of fiber optics, we had a lot of little axial lights. Axial lights were developed primarily for illuminating liquid crystal display watches. They come in a variety of sizes, but the smallest you can order is something like eighty-thousandths of an inch long. Fortunately, they can be ordered with leads attached, so it's just a matter of spreading them out carefully and soldering them to the wire. As you can imagine, there's a bit of a rejection rate there; but modelmakers have to learn to work small, and axial lights are just perfect for a lot of the things that we do. Each one has a little filament; they take three volts and they'll last a thousand hours. Then, under the table, there was a whole grid of incandescent floodlights that flared up from beneath to create sort of a glow."

Completion of the Hades setting was just cause for celebration, but the pressures of time precluded all but a brief spontaneous outburst. "The cameramen were waiting on stage for delivery,"

For closer shots, a larger-scale insert model was constructed in even greater detail. David Dryer looks over Dave Stewart's shoulder as Stewart lines up a shot on a rear projection screen built into the face of the pyramid. Ultimately, though, the live-action miniature projections — filmed months earlier during principal photography — could not be aligned to the camera's approach trajectory and the idea had to be discarded. / Model-maker Leslie Ekker created a minute replica of Tyrell's office for the insert model. / The landing platform on top featured a spired terminal built by Chris Ross, and a fleet of inch-long spinners fashioned by Leslie Ekker.

Bill George recalled, "and it was a little behind schedule. One of the modelmakers got together everyone in the shop with a pickup — I think there were six of them. The landscape was broken down and loaded into the trucks. Someone put together a makeshift flag signaling victory and we convoyed down the street. When we got to the studio parking lot we began driving around in circles and honking our horns. Everyone in the neighborhood knew Hades had arrived."

Like the pyramids it surrounded, the Hades landscape was photographed in the smoke room. The setup was not without its problems, however. The incandescent lights shining up through the model base generated such intense heat that a battery of stage fans had to be positioned on one side to circulate the air. As a result, the room heated up so drastically that the air conditioning had to be turned on — a situation which had previously been avoided for fear that the oil-based smoke might gum up the system. Fortunately, that proved not to be the case. "We used a lot of Mole smoke on those shots," said Dave Stewart, "backlit to create the atmosphere and so forth. By moving around on the miniature and rearranging our foreground pieces we were able to cut our way in and suggest sort of an extended passage over this giant industrial complex on the outskirts of the megacity. Because of the forced perspective of the miniature, we weren't able to move a *great* deal side-to-side, but we moved as much as we could and went right to the limits before perspectives changed. Then, as we work our way across Hades, we come upon those two giant pyramid structures out in the middle. For the long shots of those, Virgil Mirano shot some still transparencies of the pyramid, which we mounted on very thin neon lightboxes built by Larry Albright. Kind of an interesting technique, I thought, and not too far removed from some of the things they did on *2001* using transparencies on an animation stand — only in this case, it was a two-dimensional thing in a three-dimensional set. Anyway, as we worked our way in over Hades, we kept substituting bigger and bigger transparencies, until we got to the point where you could actually see a perspective change and we therefore needed the three-dimensional shape." The actual pyramid, of course, was totally out of scale to the Hades landscape, so it had to be shot separately — once for each of the two pyramids — and then composited optically into the Hades setting. For Stewart and his crew, this meant precise alignment of the miniatures to insure proper perspective and appropriate horizon lines, as well as scaling and calculating the computerized camera moves so that they appeared identical in the different film elements and could therefore fit together perfectly.

A key visual element in Douglas Trumbull's perception of Hades was the belching fire emitted by some of the towers. One particularly voluminous burst all but engulfs the camera as it drifts in over the hostile terrain. To achieve the flame effects, it was decided that miniature projections, aligned right to the top of the specific tower desired, would be the easiest and most effective way to go. To that end, the model shop experimented for a while with trying to incorporate rear-screen projectors into the miniature setting before David Dryer suggested that it would be far simpler just to drop a piece of white foam-core down from above, position it directly behind the designated tower, and then project the flame footage in from the front — against a background of total darkness — while the camera repeated its previously programmed motion control run. Though filmed separately from the settings to which they would later be mated in optical, the bursts of fire were calculated down to the last frame, and at appropriate moments during one of the six in-camera passes required to record the background, small lights atop the selected towers would be switched on via motion control, remain lit for a few frames to provide an interactive lighting effect on the tower and its surroundings, and then be faded out as the yet-to-be-added fireballs dissipated.

The flames themselves provided an interesting challenge. Some of the more spectacular ones were pulled from the explosive finale of *Zabriskie Point*, isolated via rotoscoping, and then projected into the Hades setting on a separate camera pass. Others were shot out in the EEG parking lot. "We used a gas jet off a welding torch," Dave Stewart explained. "It burned really hot and bright, and put out this tremendous six-foot stream of fire. Those we used primarily for the towers that are just constantly burning — burning off excess energy, I guess. Where they're going to get excess energy forty years from now I don't know, but that was part of the concept. Even though a six-foot flame is pretty impressive — especially up close — it's actually just a miniature if you're trying to create something that's coming out of a four-hundred-foot tower and it's maybe two-thirds the height of that tower. So again, it's the old formula for high-speed. My formula is you shoot as fast as the camera will go and just hope to hell it's good enough."

About midway through principal photography, first Douglas Trumbull and then Richard Yuricich began easing out of *Blade Runner* as they became more and more involved with the *Brainstorm* preproduction effort. "I must say that Ridley was very cooperative," said Trumbull, "and very understanding of the fact that I was going off and directing my own movie. As the time drew nearer, I just sort of edged myself out of the picture and even stopped going to dailies. Ridley knew that was going to happen, and he accepted it and didn't try to invade my time on my own film. Which, of course, is a tribute to Dave Dryer as well. He did a wonderful job of picking up where Dick and I left off, in understanding the approaches and actually improving on them. In fact, I think he did a better job on it than I would have done, because he's got more patience with the whole process than I have. At this point in my life, I'm just not as willing to spend all of my energies on special effects."

"At the time I took over," said Dryer, "no optical composites had yet been made. Most of the large miniatures of the pyramid had already been shot under Douglas' supervision — which was maybe a month and a half of stage shooting time. Then all the landscapes and everything from there on I was involved in. It was a pretty smooth transition — we overlapped only about a week.

Like the full pyramid, the insert model was photographed in smoke — actually low-grade diesel fuel vaporized and suspended in air — to provide natural diffusion and a realistic sense of aerial perspective. Smoke levels were regulated by means of an infrared light-sensing system which automatically triggered the smoke generator if the density began to drop. Between shots, the stage was pumped clear to facilitate setups. / Inside a smoke-proof control booth, Tama Takahashi monitors the "Icebox" motion controller during a shot.

From time to time, Richard and Douglas would get involved in a meeting here, or a little shooting there, but for the most part they were heavy into preproduction on their own project. So my job — as I saw it — was to try and execute what it was that Ridley wanted. Douglas had already laid some excellent groundwork; but after he and Richard left, a lot of new sequences came up, and we had to try and map them out to maintain the look and the feel and the texture of the live-action."

If *Blade Runner* can be said to have a central image, it must certainly be the spinner. The sleek optimism inherent in Syd Mead's basic design, all but obscured under the harsher realities of Ridley Scott's retrofitted embellishments, resulted in a vehicle that was not only functional from a story point of view, but also apropos of its intended time and environment. Moreover, in terms of continuity, it provided the film's only true bridge between the substantive reality of live-action and the ethereal world of special effects.

The full-size spinners — along with most of the other street cars designed for *Blade Runner* — were constructed by Gene Winfield, who has long specialized in building custom vehicles for Hollywood film productions, as well as other clients. Fully functional, the Winfield spinners were capable of performing most of the tasks required of them by the script — except, of course, flying. Though takeoffs and landings could be — and were — effected by means of cables attached to a huge industrial crane, actual scenes of the spinners in flight were relegated to the miniatures crew at Entertainment Effects Group.

Over a period of several months, the model shop would produce spinners in four distinct sizes — from the tiny inch-long versions built to the scale of the enlarged pyramid section, to a magnificent forty-four-inch quarter-scale replica. "The first one we built," Mark Stetson recalled, "was a fifteen-inch model — inch-to-the-foot scale. It had a full interior and a little figure inside, and it was fully lit to match the original designs — which later changed. The lighting was added to extensively later on; but the fifteen-inch model we kept to the original lighting scheme. The next one to be completed was about four inches long. It, too, had a full interior, but no figures. Unfortunately, it saw very limited use in the movie. The original plan was to build a fleet of those, so we cast up about twenty of them. Only one or two were ever finished, though, and those just sat in the background on some of the later cityscape scenes. The large spinner took the longest to complete, and that model was just a gem — really, really beautiful. It tightly matched the full-size one, including all the revisions. It had articulating wheel covers in the front pods and articulating wing section wheel covers on the rear body panels. The so-called bumper and rear body panel hinged down, and the segment above that hinged with it in synchronization. There was also plumbing built inside to connect with external liquid nitrogen tanks that were used to simulate the turbine thrusters venting out through the side and rear. Inside the cockpit, the driver's hands moved, and the driver's and passenger's heads moved — all independently; all by motion

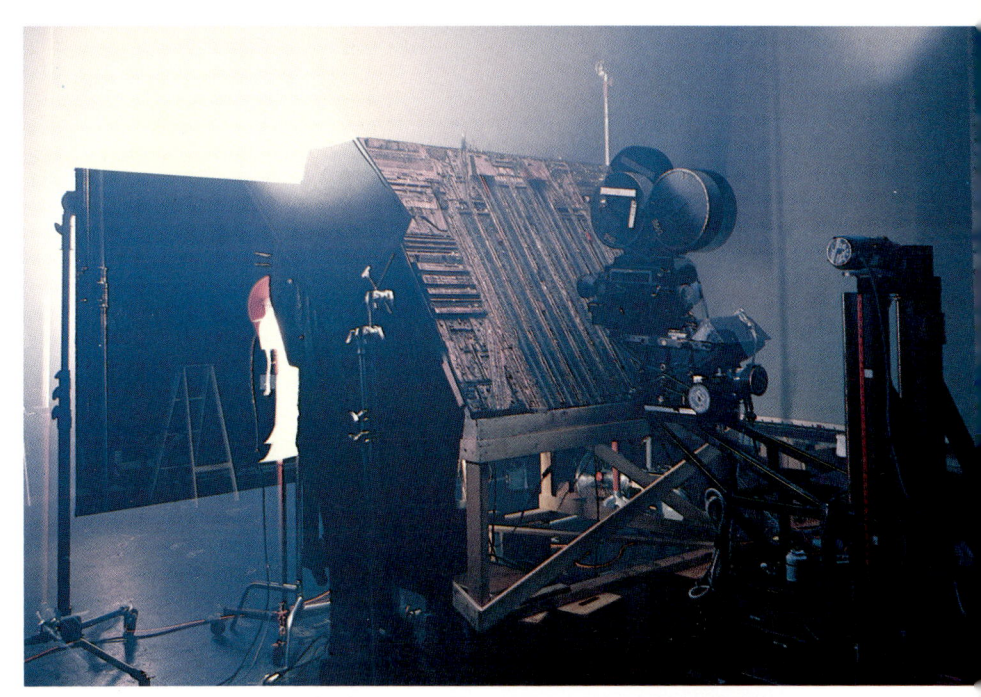

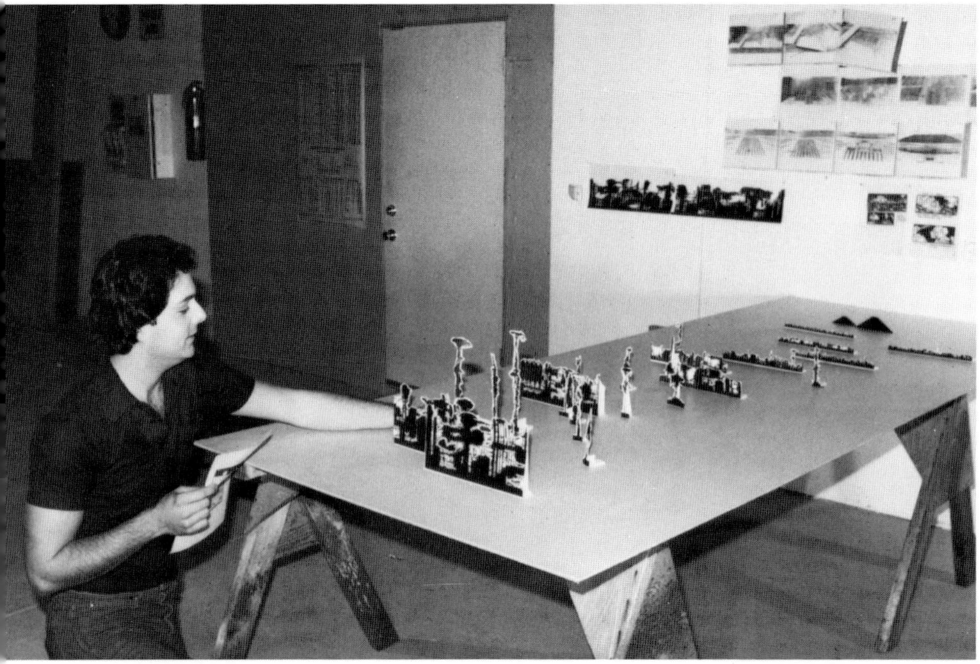

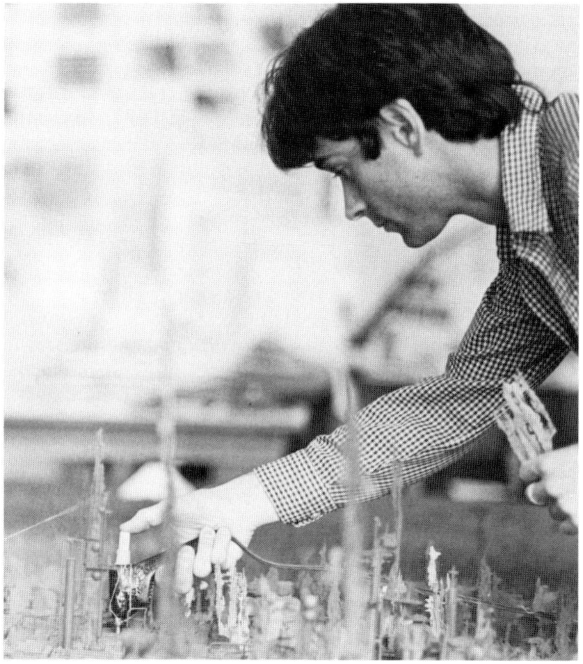

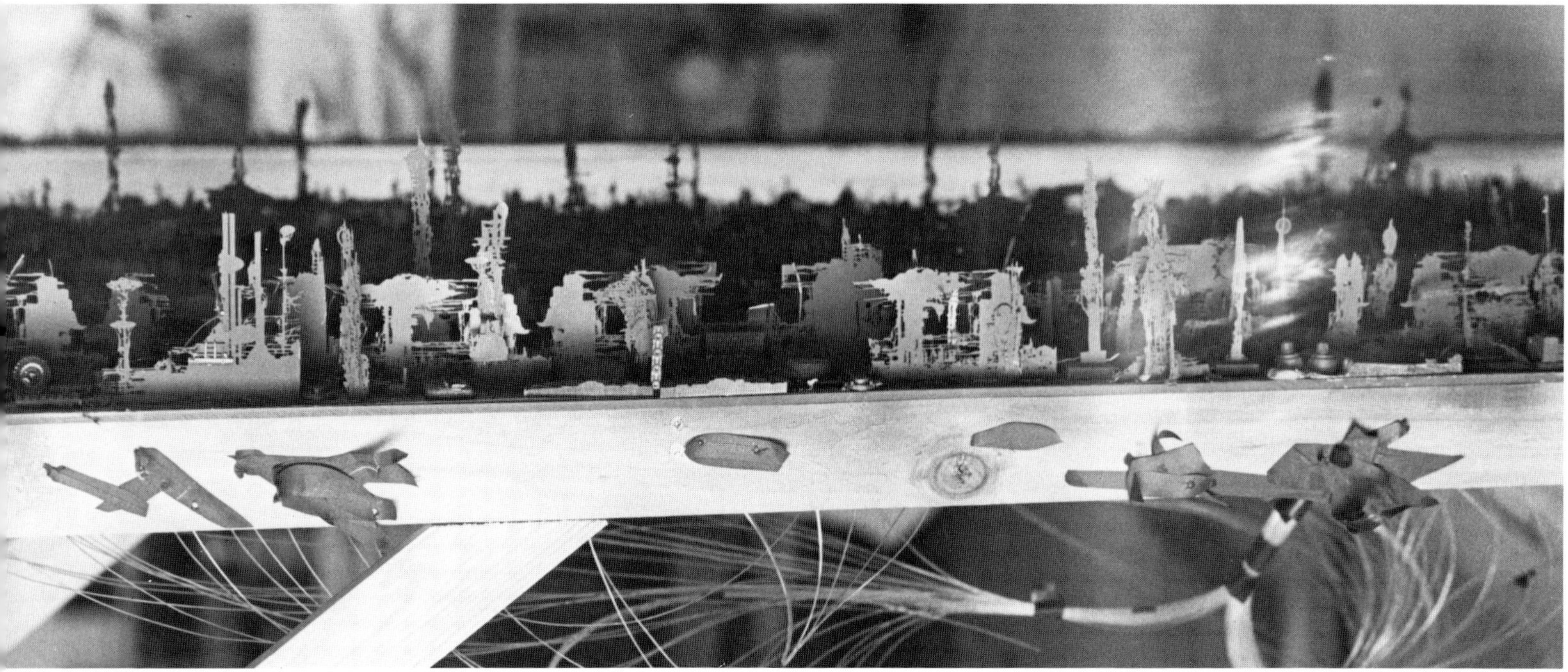

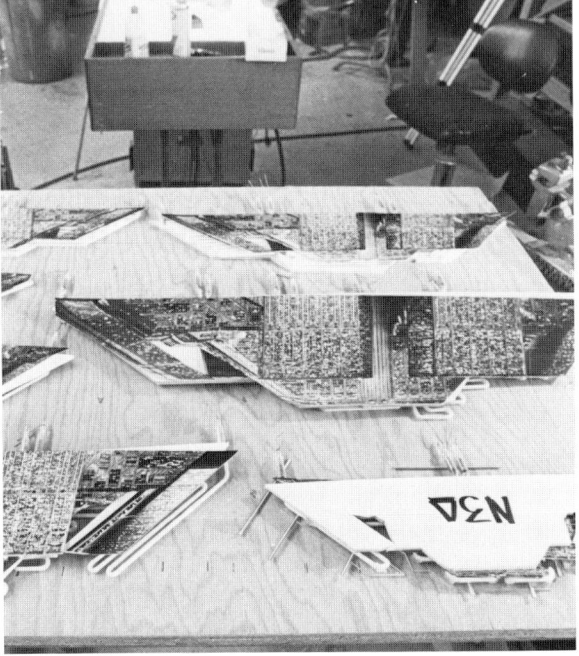

control. And, of course, it had all the lighting.

"Tom Pahk did most of the pattern work on the spinner vehicles, and Sean Casey did some absolutely phenomenal mold work. Tom started with wooden patterns, and then went through plaster molds — primarily. The canopy he vacuum-formed in one piece and the rear section of the body work was done in epoxy fiberglass laminate. Sean made up a four- or five-piece plaster mold to cast the whole midsection together; and the interior and exterior body panels were all one-piece hollow castings. On the front of the car, the pods were little hemispheres of cast epoxy fiberglass laminate; and behind the midsection were separate epoxy fiberglass laminated parts for all the wing and tail sections. The driver and passenger were sculpted in clay by Bill George and he used a lot of innovative techniques in creating clothing textures and things like that." Once the overall structure of the model was completed, it was Bill George, also, who added the all-important detailing. "The problem with the miniature spinners," he recalled, "was that, because of the slick surfaces, it was difficult to keep them from looking like toys. The only solution was to age them heavily, which we did."

On the effects stages, the miniature spinners were invariably photographed as separate, isolated film elements which would later be optically inserted into appropriate environs. "Most of the basic spinner shots required four in-camera passes," David Dryer explained. "One was a fill-light pass to give shape to the body. Then there'd be a model-light pass that would give us the headlights and strobe lights and all the other little lights in the vehicle. That had to be done separately for exposure control, because otherwise the stage lights used to illuminate the vehicle on the first pass would just totally wash out the little model lights. To create the flare effect that Ridley liked, we did a third pass on a fiber optic tube that was connected to a very bright xenon light source — we call it a post scanner setup — and that was in registration to the model and directed right toward the camera lens. Then we had a final pass on a whole series of rotating wigwag lights on top."

The wigwag lights had not been built into the already completed fifteen-inch spinner model, because at that time they had not yet been incorporated onto the full-size Winfield spinners. When they were, however, Ridley Scott wanted the miniatures to be able to produce the same effect of light beams slicing through rain and smoke. Since the large-scale spinner was already well under construction, the last-minute alteration created a temporary dilemma. "By the time Ridley added that last extra light rack," Mark Stetson recalled, "we had already pretty much filled up our entire interior space with stepper motors for all the other articulations we'd built into the model. So there was nothing we could do to motorize the spinning beacons from inside. Instead we built a nonfunctioning rack that in appearance matched the light rack on the full-size spinner. Then we built a second rack that *did* provide rotating beams — little rotating focus spots, with stepper motors and flex shafts that ran up from the rear of the model to the light rack. First the model was shot, fully stage-

Modelmaker Chris Ross positions silhouette artwork on a board for a preliminary indication of how the Hades landscape might look in forced perspective. / Leslie Ekker hot-glues etched brass refinery shapes onto a plexiglass table bed. / When properly lit, the thin, intricately-detailed brass cutouts — arranged in diminishing size from front to rear — would suggest a seemingly endless industrial wasteland. / After the etched brass pieces were affixed, seven miles of fiber optic material was threaded up from beneath to provide minute light sources for the many thousands of tower structures. / Although the original plan had been to fit small pyramid miniatures into the Hades landscape, a subsequent decision was made to produce a series of photographic transparencies which would then be mounted over thin neon lightboxes and incorporated into the setting.

lit, with the appearance rack to match the full-size spinner detail. Then the appearance rack was replaced with the 'effects' rack, and the model itself essentially became just a fixture to register the wigwag lights correctly during the second pass.''

Cameraman Don Baker, assisted by Tim McHugh, was responsible for a majority of the spinner elements. While Dave Stewart and a larger crew labored in the smoke room with the pyramid and Hades shots, Baker photographed numerous shots with the fifteen-inch spinner model on the facility's other, nonsmoke stage. ''Those were what we called the baby spinner shots,'' said Baker, ''where these guys are coming in from infinity and blasting past you at incredible speeds. I think they would have preferred them shot in smoke also, but there wasn't enough track length in the smoke room. The smoke room track was thirty feet long, but to get these high-speed zooming-to-infinity shots — even with the smaller model — we needed seventy feet of track. So I just shot them with a lot of lens flares and light tricks. They had kind of a *Close Encounters* look to them, which is pretty much what Ridley was after. He didn't like what he called the *Star Trek* look, which had very crisp, clean-looking vehicles. He wanted everything to have a little mystery of its own; and so basically, the kind of look he was after was a model that was low-lit, almost self-illuminating. And he really liked the lens flare effect that produced the big halos around the model. Those were a little bit tricky, because we had to make sure that the light source was always pointing directly at the lens, for optimum flare, even though the spinners would sometimes do ninety-degree turns. In those cases, we'd have to adjust the light during the shot, either with motion control or sometimes just by hand.''

The completed Hades landscape measured eighteen feet wide by thirteen feet deep. Although the intent had been to use the etched-brass silhouettes throughout, it was later found that three-dimensional shapes were required up front to properly sustain the illusion. Dave Stewart and David Hardberger make adjustments to some foreground pieces, while David Dryer reviews his notes on the shot. / In addition to the topside fiber optics and external lights, the miniature was lit from below with banks of floodlights that generated such intense heat that a battery of stage fans had to be emplaced to circulate the air.

Since only one miniature of any given size was available, shots requiring two or more spinners had to be photographed as separate elements and composited together in optical. One particularly complex sequence involved an early morning flight over the Hades landscape as Deckard and Gaff make their way to the Tyrell corporate headquarters. In order to create a rush hour atmosphere, Ridley Scott wanted to show numerous flying vehicles stacked in formation, darting in and out of the aerial traffic patterns and jockeying for position. To avoid having all the vehicles look exactly alike, however, executing the plan called for further involvement on the part of the miniatures crew. ''Doug asked us to come up with three different vehicles for the traffic scenes,'' Mark Stetson recalled. ''He said: 'Don't invest too much time in them. Have them armatured for maybe one position; and if you get a minute, throw a light in.' Doug makes it sound easy.''

With virtually no instructions beyond coming up with three vehicles that fit the *Blade Runner* style, Stetson turned the project over to Bill George. ''We discussed going out and buying some hand appliances and sticking some wheels on them,'' George quipped, ''but that idea was scrapped. Aside from being spinner-like, the only other description I was given was that one of the cars must look like a futuristic Ferrari. Chris Ross came up with some design sketches for me on the Ferrari; and he also sketched a hybrid of a Syd Mead design which I picked out from his book, *Sentinel*. The third vehicle was a takeoff of one of the huge trucks we had seen out on The Burbank Studios backlot. All three were built in two weeks. Later, we added more lights and different paint jobs to make them do double duty. The truck only ended up in a couple of shots, but the Ferrari and the 'Lobster' — the Syd Mead design — were used much more than originally planned. One day I was walking by Dave Dryer's office and saw the Ferrari inside. Someone had put a little bumper sticker on it that said: 'Honk If You Love Hades.' ''

Once the other unit's smoke room footage was completed, Don Baker was able to move in with the large-scale spinner model and shoot his more critical closeups in the preferred murkiness of the smoke environment. ''In the past, most of model moves we've shot have been pretty much straight in and out, with maybe just a crab move to offset them. On this film, though, we wanted to try something different — if for no other reason than to give some kind of rationale for the name 'spinner.' So we started playing around with a lot of curved moves, and we even have a couple of corkscrew-type shots where the spinner is doing over a 360-degree spiral.'' Executing such moves was an extremely complex process, however, especially since there were no curved tracks. Whatever movements were required had to be manufactured by a combination of camera and model moves on separate straight-line tracks positioned perpendicularly to each other. Due to the perceptual gymnastics involved in trying to describe compound curves in terms of straight-line trajectories — augmented with pan and tilt on the camera, plus yaw, pitch and roll on the model — led Baker to depart from the standard EEG practice of programming motion control moves manually. Manual inputting is generally effected by means of a joystick mechanism that allows the operator to program one axis of movement at a time, record that, and then play it back while a second is added — and so on until the full, desired move is in the system's memory. The Universal Hartland motion control unit Baker and McHugh were utilizing — built by Bud Elam — had the capability of inputting moves via joystick; but, unlike the older-generation Icebox, it had the alternate capability of being able to construct a move mathematically.

''It's kind of a half-human, half-computer operation,'' Baker explained. ''The computer helps a lot with the math, but there's still quite a bit of human interaction to describe the motion that you're going after. The approach is similar to joysticking in that you take your easiest motions, such as the track, and maybe a little bit of tilt — things you can describe very simply — and you program those mathematically. Then you go back and describe pan, pitch and roll — with the help of a field chart — to find out the different placements and speeds and timing. I prefer programming a move mathematically rather than by joystick recording. I just feel you have much greater control over exact placements, and a much smoother look. Joystick moves can look rather lumpy, particularly with curved moves where everything is supposed to be very, very smooth, and yet you're talking about a lot of change in directions. And you just don't have the kinds of ease-ins and ease-outs you can get doing it mathematically."

For every spinner element, of course, there needed to be a corresponding matte element. However, rather than using the standard silhouette matte technique which had sufficed admirably for the pyramid photography, an alternate frontlit approach was employed for most of the spinner mattes. In essence, instead of being photographed as dark shapes against a light background, the spinners were shot as light shapes against a dark background. "Silhouette mattes can only be used on relatively slow-moving objects," explained Dave Stewart. "When you're using motion control, even though you may be shooting at a much slower speed, you're still shooting in a 'live' way — meaning that the camera or the model, or both, are in constant movement. It's not like stop-motion where you move and shoot a frame, and then move and shoot another frame. With motion control, the move continues while the shutter's open and you get a natural streaking, so to speak. Well, the faster something moves, the more natural streaking you're going to get. So what you end up with, on any given frame, is actually a different shape — a stretched shape that varies in size, depending on its speed and how close it is to the camera. The problem with silhouette mattes is that the natural streak is recorded on the frontlit model pass — which you want — but on the matte pass, the back-lighting tends to burn it out. So what you end up with is a backlit matte that's actually a different shape and size from the frontlit model photography." To avoid this problem — and the inevitable matte lines resulting from it — the effects cameramen shifted over to frontlit mattes, bathing the miniature in light against a black background in order to preserve the same natural blur as in the primary model shot. Since the intent, however, was to create a sharply-defined counter-silhouette, and since the spinners were not inherently white, the camera crew had to cover the model entirely in white tape between the model pass and the matte pass. Then, once the matte pass was completed, the next shot was set up and its matte photographed first. Thus, the time-consuming taping ritual was limited to only one application for every two shots.

Even this technique, however, could not insure a flawless matte fit; and in many cases, if time allowed, an additional backlit silhouette matte was also shot for insurance, in order to afford maximum flexibility to the optical department. "Even though this was a more leisurely production schedule than most," said optical supervisor Robert Hall, "we were still a little cramped for time; and the stages had so many complicated setups that they couldn't very well wait until we'd finished the composites. So what we'd normally do is take the frontlit production shot and the matte and make a quick test immediately so we could screen it and tell the stage crew it was okay for them to break down the setup and go on to the next. Once we'd done that, though, we had to make it work. We'd burned our own bridges. Sometimes we'd use front-light mattes; sometimes we'd

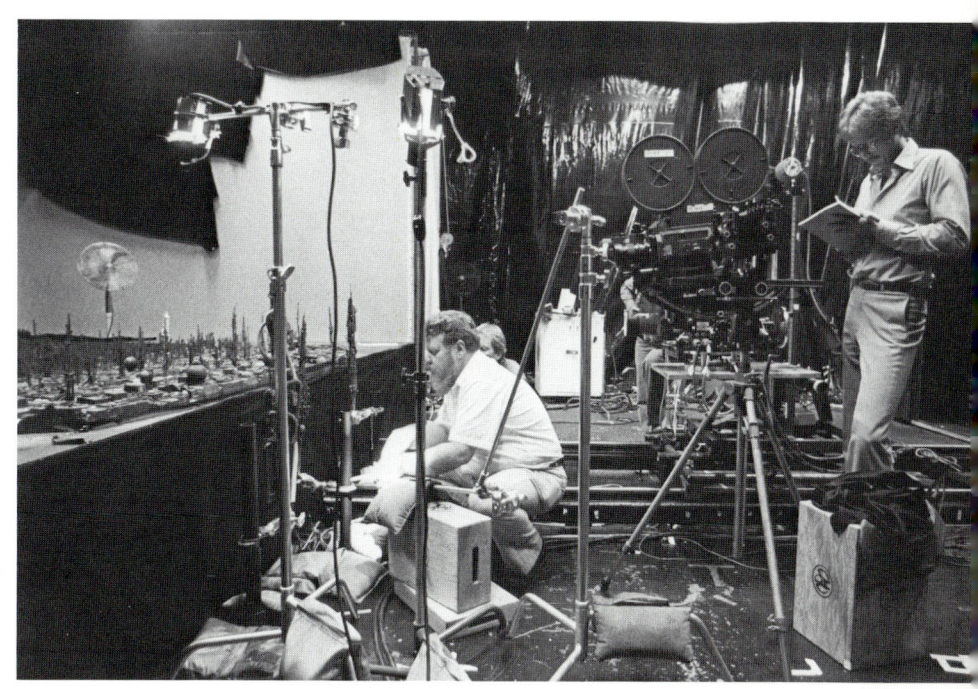

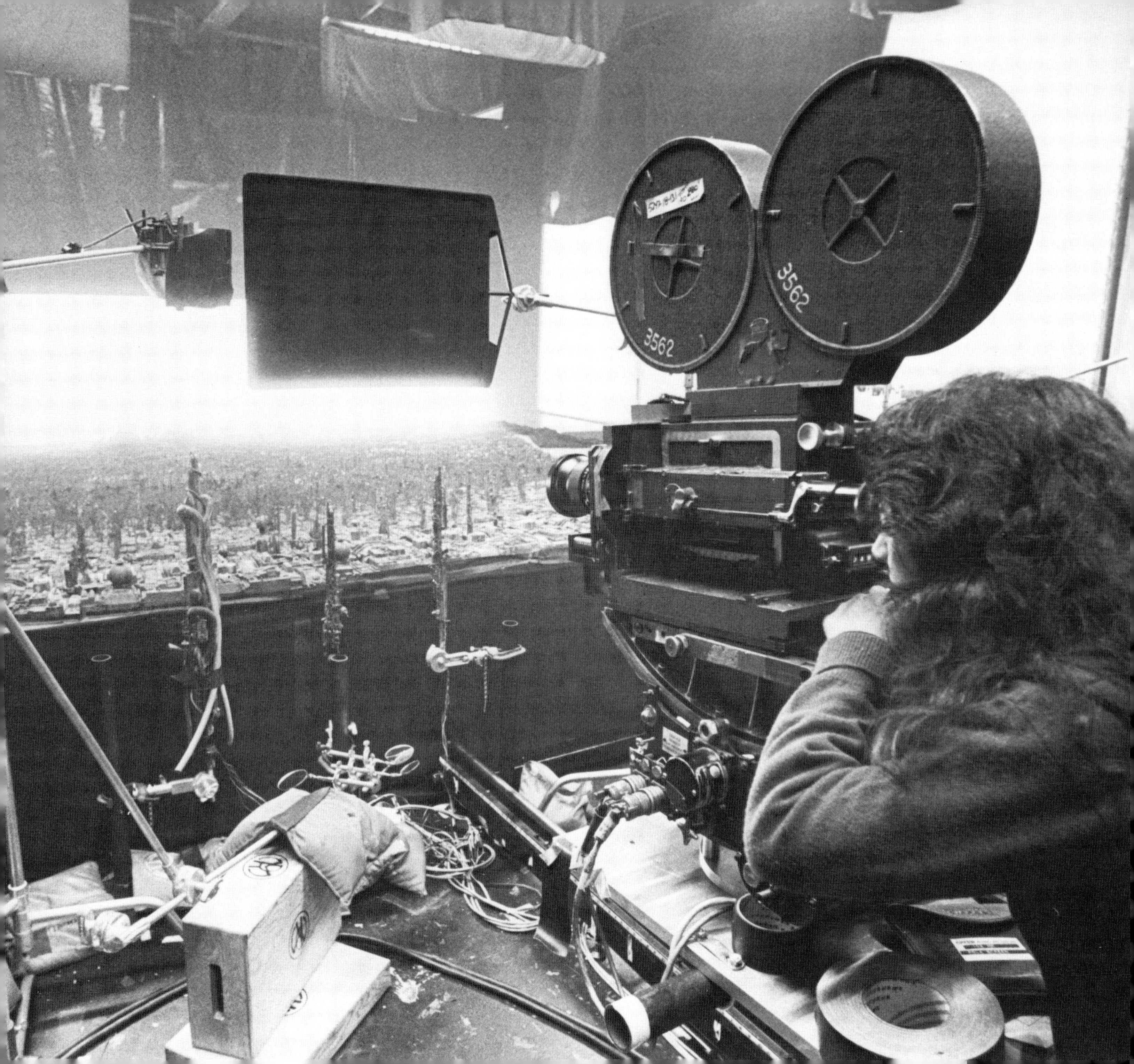
3562
3562

use back-light mattes; sometimes we'd use both together. Sometimes we didn't use *any* of them. Instead, we'd go with a straight matte pulled off the front-light production photography. We had to do that sometimes because the front-light mattes that were being shot on the stage had to be flooded with light, and as a result, the image tended to be swollen. If it wasn't *too* bad, we could sometimes shrink them down — but that didn't always work. So what we'd do instead was make registered color prints from the production photography and generate our black-and-white hi-cons from those. Those were particularly useful on the spinner shots, and we often combined them with the regular front-light mattes to help preserve the flares and some of the other things that might otherwise have been contaminated out. So basically, we used all the tried-and-true methods — and when those didn't work, we flew by the seat of our pants."

One of the most challenging aspects of the optical involvement was the insertion of spinners and other miniature elements into appropriately smog-laden background plates — without having them come out looking like cutouts. "A lot of effects houses make a mistake when they have a flying object," said David Dryer. "As it flies away and gets smaller, it tends to be just as sharp and just as clear as it was when it was right up close. That's not exactly a startling revelation, but it *is* something that seems to happen a lot. To get around that, we worked out a series of formulas for fading out background mattes and fading in contamination. So as the spinner — or whatever else it may be — flies away, it appears to be gaining aerial perspective; and we can even take it down to the point where it disappears altogether. At the same time, you fade down your overall top-light exposure, too — so it gets dimmer and dimmer and eventually just goes away. This gives a much more realistic look. Otherwise, these things look like postage stamps stuck in the shot."

"Matte density was always a major concern," Bobby Hall confirmed. "In order to get the nice soft-edged mattes that really make things fit together nicely, you have to get just the right balance between your holdout matte and your cover matte — and that comes largely from experimentation and testing. Normally we'd use the very lightest holdout matte we could and still get away with it. A lot of times we were just on the very ragged edge of bleeding through. But that's what you have to do; and after awhile, you generally develop a feel for it. The toughest thing from our point of view, I think, was lineup — especially with the kind of matting system we use at EEG where the primary photography and the mattes are photographed separately at different times. Even the slightest variance can create major problems when it comes time to fit all the elements together. One of our biggest challenges was in the shots where we had four or five ships flying over a daylight Hades background. I'm telling you, those mattes had to be *exactly* perfect — and some of them weren't. Some of them didn't follow correctly, and we had to do a lot of cheating on those in lineup to make sure that they at least fit at the most critical spots."

Bridging the gap between miniature work and live-action is always one of the crucial elements in special effects; and so for the interior spinner shots in *Blade Runner*, special pains were taken to insure that interior and exterior imagery corresponded precisely. "We always try to work to a certain level of perfection," said Dave Stewart. "Traditionally, most cockpit-type shots are done in front of a blue screen or something, and then the backgrounds are put in optically. We did that on *Star Trek* in the travel pod, and it's all over the place in *Star Wars* and *Empire* and films like that — so it's pretty much a classic approach. It works very well with space movies because there's nothing but blackness out there, and maybe a few stars. But we were doing daylight-type stuff, or scenes with lots of bright lights outside, and we wanted to make it look like it was actually coming through the canopy with all the natural distortion that it would actually have. So months after the principal photography was finished, we brought the full-size cockpit down here and lined the camera up to identically match the live-action shots — only this time without the actors. There was one shot with the actors in the foreground, but it was a locked-down shot and their heads didn't cross over into the actual windshield area, so that was no problem. We put a back projection screen on the other side of the canopy and just projected in some miniature composite scenes that we'd shot — like flying across Hades. Then we could add smoke gags and rain and whatever else we wanted and it really looked like we were photographing something outside the canopy. Plus, with the rain and smoke and stuff, we didn't have to worry about whether we were losing image quality through the back projection, because it was all distorted anyway. We had another shot — looking out the front — where this spinner comes flying in over the top of the one we're in, and the light from the screen naturally fell into the cockpit and momentarily reflected off all the instruments — just like it would." For other scenes where the camera was positioned outside the cockpit looking down through the canopy at Deckard and Gaff, the stage crew took the white dome shape that had been used as the vacuum-form windshield pattern for the largest of the spinner miniatures, aligned it precisely to the live-action shot, and then projected cityscape footage onto it. This footage — reverse-printed to go backwards, as it actually would — was then double-exposed directly over the live-action to create a realistic reflection effect on the glistening canopy.

Other spinner interiors — looking out the front of the craft from a position directly behind its two occupants — presented an added complexity in that they showed the complete instrument panel, including a video monitor with six smaller readout screens adjacent to it. The simplest means of filling those screens would have been to rear-project the desired imagery during principal photography. The intent, however, was to have the vidscreens reflect what was also being seen outside the windshield — and since that footage was still months away from the live-action shooting, a decision was made to insert the readouts optically. Therefore, during principal photography, the screens

Tama Takahashi lines up a shot on the Hades landscape. In order to suggest a lengthy passage over the industrial complex, successive shots in the sequence were photographed from slightly different angles to conceal the fact that the same terrain was being used throughout. Early shots featured the smallest pyramid transparencies, which were then replaced with progressively larger ones as the camera cut its way in. The three towers in the foreground were mounted independent of the setting and could thus be rearranged and positioned in such a way that the camera could fly right past them.

A spinner rockets in over the Hades landscape toward the Tyrell headquarters. Several in-camera passes were required to build up the basic background image against which the flying vehicle — separately photographed — was matted. Flames emanating from various stacks were also shot as independent elements by lowering a white card into the Hades set, positioning it behind the desired tower, and then projecting pyrotechnic footage in from the front as the camera repeated its motion control pass. The pyramids were backlit photographic transparencies incorporated into the setting. / Closer views employed the eight-foot pyramid miniature which had to be photographed from different angles and composited together to look like two separate structures.

were simply whited over so the optical department could pull a matte without difficulty. What was overlooked, however, was the fact that when Gaff made a hard turn, the steering mechanism crossed over into the screen area — which presented Glenn Campbell with his major rotoscope nightmare on the film.

"Optical was able to isolate everything around the cockpit, but they were not able to get rid of the blinking lights that were on the steering control which moved in front of the six smaller screens. And, of course, the guy who's playing Gaff is really getting into it. I could just see Ridley Scott sitting off-camera going: 'Look like you're driving — move your hands.' So he was moving all over the place — blocking off all the screens, blurring. Plus there were some grips outside waving spotlights around so there'd be some interactive lighting; and every once in awhile, one of the lights would cross over the entire panel and everything would be lost — even the lines on the screen. So it took about a full week of roto and inking to get the mattes we needed — six hundred and sixty-some frames. It was pretty awful. It did give me an opportunity to try something I've wanted to do for years, though, which was to use various graduated-tone gray markers to delineate the edges during the blur sequences. Anything that was definitely solid, of course, I would just ink in. But in those places where he'd move his hands and everything would go bananas, I'd take those gray markers and do a graduated shading so there'd be some transparency on the final matte. Otherwise, it was all or nothing. It's not something you'd want to do on every shot; but in a case like this, where it was only blurred on occasion and you knew it was going to be silhouetted in front of the screen where your eye would naturally be drawn to it, I thought it would be worth the extra bother."

Once the articulate roto matte was completed, optical had only to insert the appropriate vidscreen imagery. "We wanted a computer representation of what we were seeing outside the window," said David Dryer. "So what we did was take our footage of the miniature background we were projecting outside, and we made two positive-negative hi-con prints and then offset them slightly to get an etch-line representation that actually vibrated a little like video. Then, over that, we had our Compsy machine shoot kind of an abstract tunnel that multiplanes in space and rotates. So as the spinner is turning, the tunnel is turning; and then it lines up square and takes you on down the street."

Even though they were photographed as isolated elements, the spinners, quite naturally, needed an environment in which to operate. And since the story was both futuristic and urban-oriented, a convincing extension of the 21st-Century ground-level settings erected on The Burbank Studios backlot had to be created as well in miniature. That project, at least initially, fell into the hands of Wayne Smith. Smith, who had gotten his first taste of filmmaking as art director for *Silent Running*, had also been involved with several subsequent Trumbull projects, but had most recently come from a supervisory post at the defunct Universal Hartland facility. The model shop had already been set up by Mark Stetson, who at that point was still acting as Greg Jein's designated representative. When it became apparent, however, that Jein's commitment to *One From the Heart* was going to be long-term and all-consuming, Wayne Smith was brought in to fill the supervisory gap. "Wayne and I concurred and collaborated on everything," Stetson explained, "but Wayne, as shop coordinator, was more involved with design and planning and budgeting, and really forecasting the way the project was going to go. I, on the other hand, was more involved with the day-to-day responsibilities of running the shop. The first thing Wayne did when he came on was to evaluate the project; and once he had, he told Doug and Richard that they really ought to double or triple their intended expenditures for the model shop. He was pretty close to being right."

"By the time I got there," said Smith, "the one area no one seemed to have dealt with yet was the cityscape stuff; and we knew that was going to be a big problem down the road. There hadn't been any design work done on that, and since the other areas seemed to be moving along pretty well, I decided to direct my attention primarily to that. Although we were reporting directly to Doug, we had some early meetings with Ridley and Larry Paull. From those we were able to get a pretty good feel for the character of the film, which was shaping up to be kind of a mix of the old and the new, but with a heavy art deco influence. So we tried to capture that flavor as well. I went out with a still camera and drove all over Los Angeles taking pictures of buildings that were representative of that style. From there we essentially copied certain buildings, doctoring them up and adding other bits of detailing that we liked. And, of course, since we wanted to match the exterior street scenes, our buildings had to have the same retrofitted industrial look, with tubing and vents and various kinds of boxes and things all over them.

"The idea was to make the buildings as versatile as possible so we could redress them and rearrange them and use them over and over again — because the budget was really quite tight. At that point, the sequence was designed in short cuts — maybe four or five seconds — so we could do that. There were no long, panning shots where you'd need to have a really huge set. But it *was* being shot in 65mm and there were some close flybys, so the buildings we did make would have to be fairly large and well-detailed. At Greg Jein's suggestion, we decided on a one-inch scale for the really close stuff, which was helpful because that's doll house scale. I didn't realize it at the time, but there's quite a substantial doll house industry, and lots of small outfits make tons of stuff in that scale — from furniture and accessories on up to windows and siding and molding and all kinds of things. As a result, we were able to buy an awful lot of what we needed already made. Most of the buildings were either two- or three-sided, and the largest of them were about eight to ten feet high — so they pretty much filled up the whole shop. We built five or six of them in the one-inch scale, and we made some others in half-inch scale and quarter-inch scale. Beyond that the scale didn't really matter. Then these would all be arranged in diminishing perspective, lit with a lot of little lights, and filmed

CINEFEX 9 ▶ 37

38 ◀ CINEFEX 9

in the smoke room."

Largely through the efforts of construction foreman Jerry Allen — assisted by Vance Frederick — the buildings were fleshed out in record time, and then detailed, inside and out, by Mike McMillen and Bill George. The entire project took only about three or four months. Then the models sat around the shop for a few weeks waiting for the smoke room crew to catch up. In the meantime, Wayne Smith left the *Blade Runner* company to take another assignment, leaving the follow-on involvement to Mark Stetson. "In the original plan," said Stetson, "the cityscapes were to have had fairly limited use. The idea was to use them for a continuation shot of the spinner takeoff — which was done live on the full-size set — and then just have the spinner fly through some of the lower buildings and do the rest with matte paintings. When it came time for the first shot, we hauled all the stuff over to the stage and spent about three days getting it set up. I thought it looked *fantastic* — we all did. But then Ridley came in and took a look at it and said it was too limited. So: 'Mark, we need a new city.' Of course, at this point it was really a rush. We went back to the shop and took any large shape we could find that had some interest to it and dressed it out as a building. I bought some Sonotube — which is kind of heavy-duty cardboard tubing that's used at construction sites as a form for pouring concrete. They made rather nice large architectural shapes. Then we got some overhead lighting grids, punched them up with tape real quickly and put them in the back of some of the shots. We also had a number of lightboxes with grids on the front, which Wayne had had the foresight to design and have built. Those we taped over to create various window sizes and stacked them up into giant towers. At this point, we were starting to get a little bit more of the expanse that Ridley wanted. Then Dave Dryer began getting the feeling we were limiting ourselves by working on these large buildings with full interiors, and that we were actually getting better scale suggestion in the smaller models. He suggested that we go back to the pyramid idea of just using little bits of light to indicate rooms. So we cut down our scale. We started building five-foot buildings, with all kinds of stuff sprouting all over them. A couple of guys on the crew — being science fiction fans — had built fairly large replicas of spacecraft from other movies, and so we have Jon Roennau's *Dark Star* and Bill George's *Millennium Falcon* standing on end in there, and dressed up with towers and stuff like that."

Even though neon lighting was to be a dominant motif in the live-action city sets, it was determined fairly early on that miniature neon — used to considerable effect in *Close Encounters* and *1941* — was simply too rich for the *Blade Runner* budget. As a result, the light sources used throughout were predominantly incandescent. With Virgil Mirano's assistance, however, the appearance of neon was still incorporated into the miniature cityscape. "At every opportunity," Mirano explained, "I'd go up to the live-action *Blade Runner* street set on the nights they were shooting, for the purpose of providing visual material to aid our modelmakers. Even though set design sketches and illustrations are suggestions of the filmic reality, in fact the actual look is constantly undergoing interpretation and modification throughout the progress of the shooting. Therefore, it was important to maintain an updated visual record, which would then become a production tool for us in our effort to duplicate aspects of that live-action reality in miniature. Well, the most significant payoff was that I shot all these wonderful neon signs that were all over the street set — mostly graphics and Oriental characters. These stills were then blown up to a variety of scaled transparent chromes which, when backlit, became miniature cityscape signing, consistent with the look of the live-action street scenes."

Among the most striking additions to the cityscape concept, though, were the gigantic animated billboards installed on whole sides of certain buildings. "Ridley's view of the future," David Dryer explained, "was that media will be everywhere, and giant billboards, maybe a hundred stories high, will be illuminated series of maybe thousands of television tubes, all interconnected and computer-controlled to play out an advertising message of one sort or another. The screens were built directly onto some of the buildings, and the screen surfaces were plastic panels covered with a series of bumps that were silvered on the top and black in the valleys. Thus, any image projected onto it from the front would be reflected back off the silver but absorbed by the black, and the result was that it looked like a matrix of tiny TV tubes."

The effects unit was responsible not only for developing the basic approach to the video billboards, but also for devising and filming the various commercial messages which would be projected onto them. With thirteen years' experience as a director of television commercials, David Dryer was more than qualified to handle the task. Working closely with him on the project was animation supervisor John Wash, a specialist in motion graphics and a fellow veteran of countless commercial spots. Like the predominant street-level advertising, the billboards promoted both futuristic products and those carried over from the present. "One of the viewpoints taken by the film," said Wash, "is that Japanese and Hispanic cultures will have risen to the forefront by 2020. So in keeping with that idea, Dave shot a lot of live-action material — geisha girls popping gum into their mouths, and things like that. Later we'd add graphics to the live-action and then project it up onto these giant billboard-type things — so as you're flying through the city, there'd be these huge faces looming out at you. It was pretty impressive. Some of the more involved concepts were worked out beforehand by Dave Dryer, but others were just straight graphics — like RCA and Coca-Cola logos and things like that — and it would be left pretty much up to me to design something apropos using fairly traditional backlit animation techniques. The idea was kind of a futuristic Times Square concept. Logos would reveal and then disappear, and letters would come on — nothing very complicated. The primary objective was just to maintain a sense of graphic integrity. The commercials were being projected onto textured screens,

Bill George's flying truck passes in front of the pyramid as the camera moves in on the early morning setting. / For a connective shot intended to establish the spatial relationship between the city and Hades, a detailed rooftop miniature was constructed and photographed with the refinery setting in the background. / David Hardberger, assisted by Susan Sitnek, lines up the rooftop shot — which ultimately was deleted from the film.

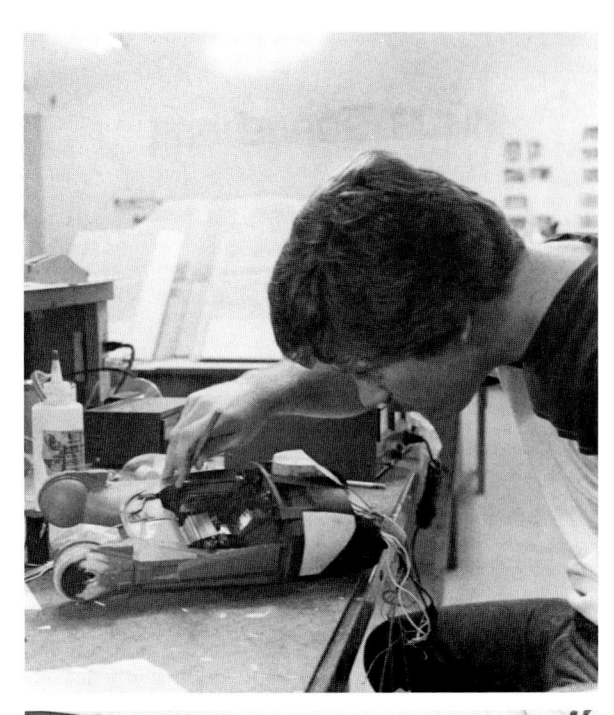

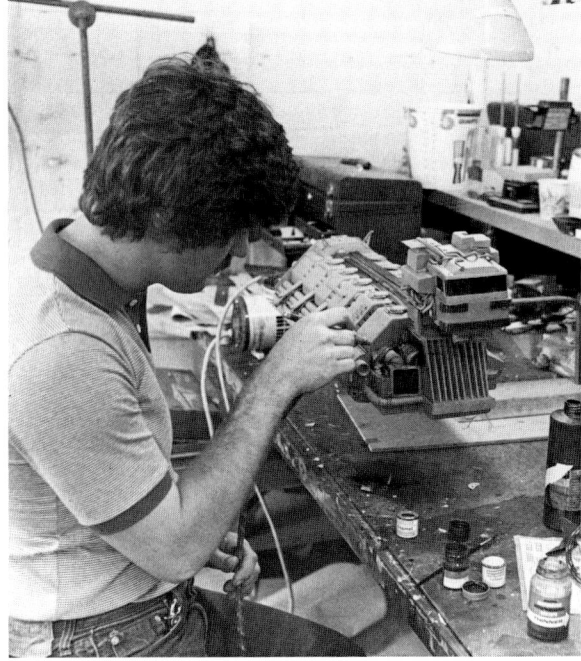

Spinner models were built in four different scales, ranging from one inch to forty-four inches in length. Bill George incorporates miniature detailing into the cockpit area of a fifteen-inch version which was used primarily for scenes in which spinners had to fly past the camera and zoom off into the distance — or vice versa. / In addition to working on the police spinners, George fabricated three other flying vehicles — including a modular truck he extrapolated from a full-size street vehicle used during the live-action shoot. / Tom Pahk was responsible for the basic spinner shape. / Pahk and George at work on the largest of the spinner models. / For it, Bill George fashioned two human figures whose arms and heads could move via motion control.

which tended to break up the image in interesting ways; but the image still had to be fairly strong graphically to maintain its readability. One of the major story points that we wanted to emphasize in some of the advertising was the concept of off-world colonization, where people were being encouraged to escape the decay and crime and congestion of earth and emigrate to the great suburbia of the future — which in this case happened to be on Jupiter or some place like that. A big gag we put in concerning off-world was the availability of thirty-six percent loans. We all thought that was pretty funny, but just about everybody who's seen it thinks we may have underestimated a bit." Like the already-completed Esper footage, the customized commercials were shot in standard 35mm format; and as Don Baker had done earlier, Glenn Campbell accomplished the cel-by-cel backlit animation on a rented Oxberry at Nick Vasu's.

After extensive urban renewal, the renovated cityscapes met with Ridley Scott's approval, and photography began in earnest on the smoke stage. Even so, every setup seemed to have its own unique demands. Many of them ricocheted back to the model shop. "Even though we were given ample time to build the spinner and the pyramid," Bill George commented, "we were often asked to produce what I called 'models in minutes.' Over on the stage they'd be setting up a shot and they'd suddenly decide they needed a bridge or a new megastructure or something, and the model shop would be asked to provide it — usually within a couple of hours. Since there was obviously no time to order materials, it was like improv-modelmaking. The 'sushi bar' was one of our first improv-projects. It was supposed to represent a large section of one of the towers in Hades, with a restaurant and a gas station, and it was constructed all from loose scraps and things I could find in the shop — including an unsuspecting Sparklett's water bottle."

"We became kind of an emergency response force," Mark Stetson added, "and we got pretty good at it. I kept carrying stuff over there as fast as they could dream it up. We made bridges and extra buildings and signs — lots and lots of signs. We had a call for one that was for a special shot where Deckard's looking up at Leon's hotel, and it has a big 'YUKON' on it. We built that overnight. Bill George framed in the letters, and about four or five of us stayed and divvied them up and just started plugging in little tiny lightbulbs — about five hundred of them. Threw it all together and got it over to the camera by next morning. Anything that looked even remotely architectural, we'd use. In fact, it's really surprising how indicative you can be for background stuff, as long as you have some interesting, scale-establishing items in the foreground. You can really get away with a lot in the smoke room. For one shot, we even took the pyramid — which they'd already finished with — changed the color on it, took the buttresses off and added some pillars. That was going to be for a separate element, and then that element was going to be inverted so it would look like a building that kind of mushroomed out — and it was going to go in as part of another shot."

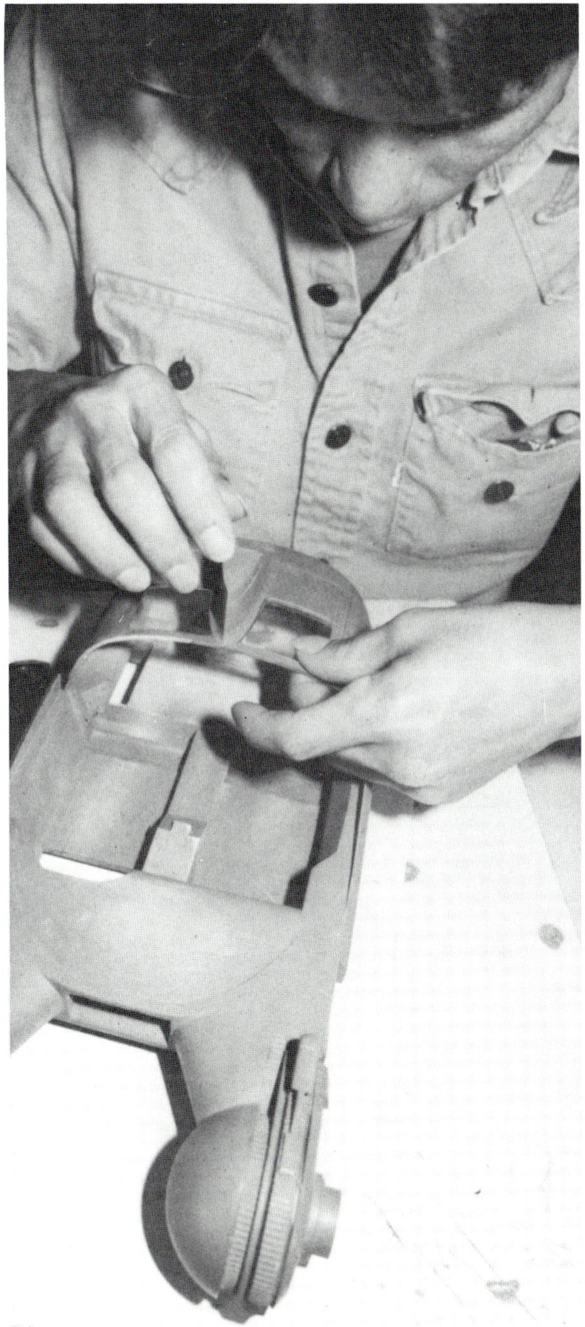

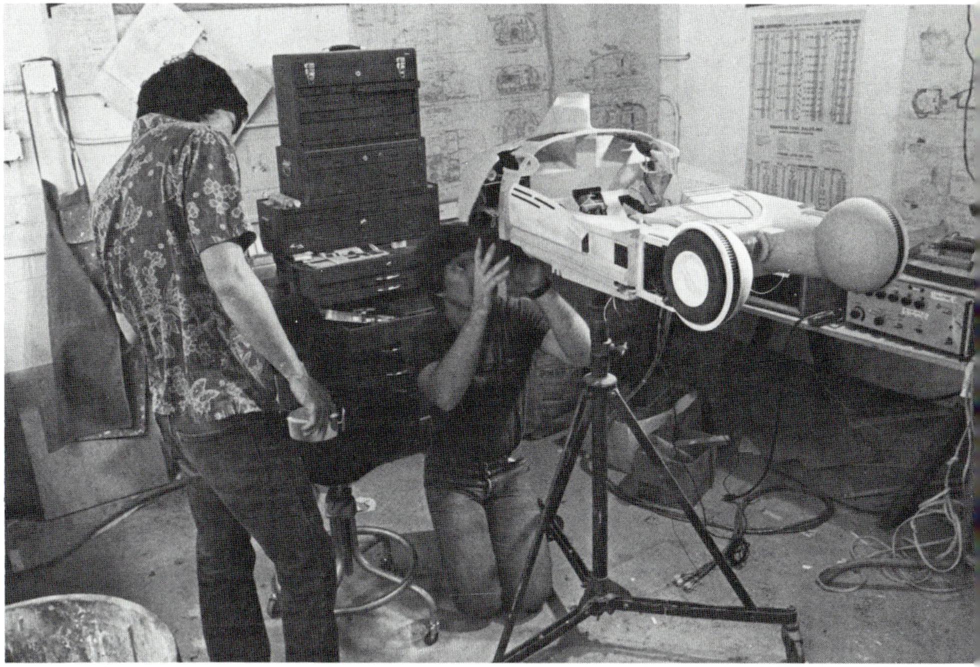

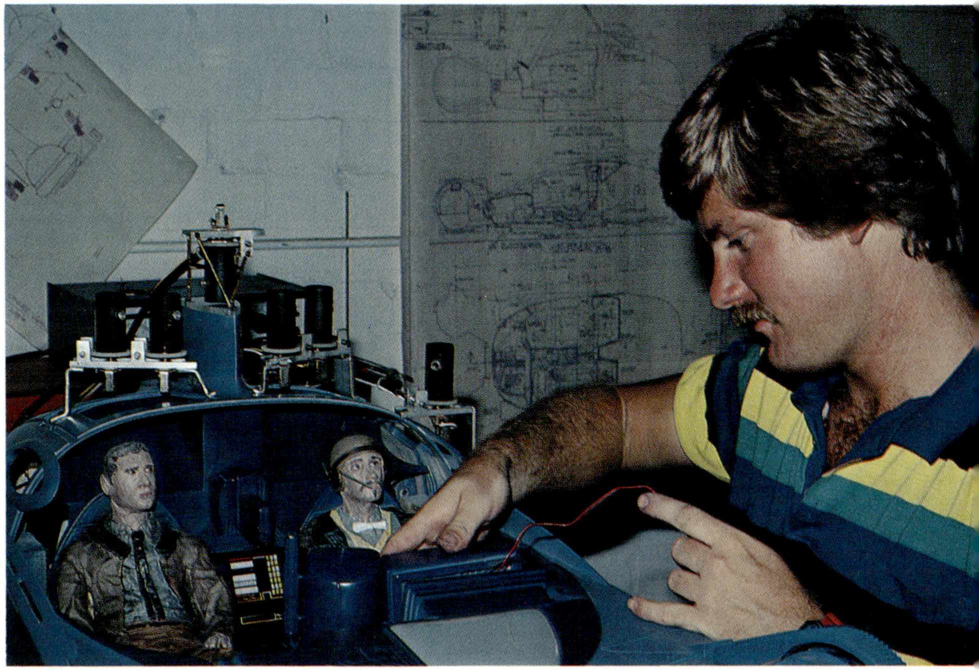

42 ◄ CINEFEX 9

All did not go well with the revitalized pyramid, however. "We were doing everything we could to make it look different," Dave Stewart explained, "and one of the things we were doing was using a longer lens to change perspectives and so forth on the thing. The problem was that being a long lens, it was also slower; and so the exposure time was much longer. We had it lit from the inside with a 5K lamp, and it sat there in the smoke room for about four hours and just finally caught on fire. It was funny, in a way, because the cameraman, John Seay, didn't even notice at first. He was sitting out in the booth with his computer, you know; and every once in a while he'd go in and check on things. Well, at the time, Rob Hummel happened to be giving a tour of the facility, and so he went into the room and then came over to the booth and said: 'John, is the pyramid supposed to be on fire?' For all he knew, maybe we were shooting a burning building. John sat there for a moment or two waiting for the punchline, and then realized he was serious and ran in with a fire extinguisher and put it out. So it was no big problem — except, of course, it destroyed the miniature. Being made out of plastic, it tended to melt right down. Fortunately, it was a throwaway shot, more or less — nothing we couldn't live without."

One of the most elaborate sequences in the film involved Deckard's spinner spiraling in for a landing on top of the police precinct building — a short series of shots which required the construction of an altogether separate multi-structure setting. "We treated that as a special model project," said Mark Stetson, "and not part of the overall cityscape. The design was a little more carefully controlled than the other stuff because it had to correspond — a least to some extent — with some live-action that had been shot at Union Station. So the art deco theme was established. Ridley had kind of an infatuation with the Chrysler Building and wanted it in the city somehow; but at that point we just didn't have enough left in the budget to tackle a replica building like that. But we did have the precinct station yet to go, so we gave it that whole art deco Chrysler Building theme — vaulting arches and stuff like that." The precinct building was only part of the setup, however. Other buildings had to be manufactured outright or modified from existing structures.

Dave Stewart considered the master approach shot his most difficult assignment on the film. "At first it seems like a point-of-view shot from their spinner because we're traveling along — like a helicopter shot — across rooftops and so forth to get to the precinct building. But then, two or three seconds before everything comes to a stop, the spinner flies in past camera from below and starts going into a spiraling landing pattern. So what we had was the camera coming in and rotating in a clockwise direction, and then the spinner coming in on a curved trajectory and rotating on itself in a counterclockwise direction — and that involved motion controlling just about all the different axes we had."

The most peculiar aspect of the shot, however, was the orientation of the cityscape. "The miniature alone took a week just to set up," David Dryer revealed, "because it was tilted over at about a forty-five degree angle so the camera could get the aerial view. Also, it was a real job lining it up in the camera because we were using a 28mm lens — which is really a wide lens for 65mm — and each building had to be individually aligned in a compromised position so it appeared correct to the barrel distortion of the lens. As a result, no two buildings were at the same angle. Then we had to go in and fill in all the areas down below, so we wouldn't see the stage floor."

"One of the things we did," Dave Stewart elaborated, "was to take part of the blowup section of the pyramid that had the motorized elevators in it and lay it out on the ground as part of a train station, or something, way off in the distance. Then we glued a couple of baby spinners to it — so if anybody happens to notice, there are little things moving around on the street down there. Lots of buildings were created practically on the spot — taking faces off this building and adding them to that. Off in the distance, we had to create buildings that didn't exist — or at least a representation of more structures further in the background. For these we used some four-by-eight pieces of black foam-core and put little pieces of white tape on them. Lighting it all became a real nightmare."

Once the setup was completed, it took another full week just to shoot it. "There were eight in-camera passes, just for the miniature background," David Dryer continued, "and many of those took hours on end to expose. The first pass was a fill light pass to give shape and form to the buildings. Then we had other passes for the miniature light sources — all the fiber optic windows and such. There must have been two thousand of them. We also used dental mirrors to reflect in little pools of light to bring out certain details. Then all the street signs and giant ads clinging to the sides of buildings had to be projected in separate passes in order to control the exposures. In some cases, the miniature setup itself was so confining that we had to use mirrors to get the projected images in, and then try to keep those out of the shot — which was no easy task since the camera literally starts ninety degrees on its side and then flies in and rotates around and looks straight down on top of the buildings. And you can see *everything*. We had elevators and radar antennas on the roofs and little vehicles moving around down on the street — all motion controlled. And there were little motion controlled light beams coming up through the smoke. And that was just the background. On top of that, we had our large model of the spinner flying in very close to the frame and circling down, and there were six additional passes just for it."

From his perspective as chief cameraman for the spinner elements, Don Baker found the master precinct landing among his most complex tasking as well. While most of his shots required on the average of four hours' worth of programming and motion testing, the precinct approach required eight. A later shot in the sequence called for the liquid nitrogen retrojet effect as the spinner settles down on its rooftop landing pad. This required yet another in-camera pass, since the nitrogen venting had to be backlit for maximum effect and shot at twelve frames

The large-scale closeup spinner — photographed primarily by Don Baker and assistant Tim McHugh — was an exact replica of its full-size counterpart, complete with articulating wheel covers, liquid nitrogen exhaust ports and rotating beacons. / To insure that natural motion blur was present on both production and matte passes, the spinner matte elements were photographed frontlit, rather than backlit as the pyramid and cityscapes had been. In order to get a clean frontlit matte, however, the model had to be completely covered with white tape. Although most of the production passes were filmed in smoke, the matte passes were not. / A rush hour traffic scene over the Hades landscape involved painstaking compositing of numerous separate spinner elements.

per second.

Though it is the dimensional cityscapes, with their constantly shifting perspectives and aerial activity, that give *Blade Runner* its most awesome visual moments, the really expansive vistas called for yet another medium. For these, the effects unit turned to master matte artist, Matthew Yuricich. An Oscar winner for his work on *Logan's Run*, and a subsequent nominee for *Close Encounters of the Third Kind*, Matthew Yuricich is a widely respected painter who has been expanding the filmmaker's palette since the early Fifties. It was then, under the aegis of M-G-M's innovative matte department maestros, artist Lee LeBlanc and cameraman Clarence Slifer, that Yuricich learned and mastered the art of painting to intermediate duplicating stock rather than original color negative. Entertainment Effects Group is a staunch advocate of the duping technique, believing that — at least on 65mm film stock — the process produces an image comparable to original negative, but with considerably more flexibility. Because of the complexities involved, however, the technique is all but defunct, and aside from Matthew Yuricich and his protege, Rocco Gioffre, no one else in the business employs it.

While no one can challenge the quality inherent in first generation effects work, the time-honored approach of painting to original negative does have limitations. First, the matte shot must be very thoroughly planned out in advance of principal photography, and a specific matte line must be determined and a matte positioned in front of the camera to mask those portions of the frame where the painting is to appear. A determination must also be made as to whether a hard- or soft-edged matte is desired, and the mask thus positioned accordingly. Generally, several approved live-action takes must be recorded as insurance against possible problems in the postproduction phase. These takes are then held in a latent state until the painting can be added. Paintings are normally done on glass and then wedged to extra footage off the tail end of the latent take to determine appropriate exposure, color intensity and alignment of the two elements. Once a wedge is approved, the painting is then photographed on the same piece of film as the latent live-action take to produce a final first generation composite. Other compositing techniques, such as rear projection and front projection of the live-action element, can provide greater flexibility with regard to matte line placement and element positioning since neither has to be specifically determined on the set. They have a corresponding disadvantage, however, in that the live-action portions of the frame no longer have the pristine quality of first generation imagery. Other drawbacks include the possibility of distortion, diffusion or other aberrations caused by the process screens themselves, plus the fact that they are duped onto original negative — rather than a stock intended for that purpose — which tends to increase contrast and alter color. EEG's use of Eastman 5243 color intermediate stock — which, depending upon the processing chemicals used, will produce either an interpositive or a dupe negative — eliminates the latter two problems altogether since it is intended specifically for duplicating purposes. The end result is still a second generation live-action image, but the fact that the compositing is done in 65mm and then reduced — generally to 35mm anamorphic — eliminates virtually all loss in quality.

The EEG matte stand, built originally for *Close Encounters* but refined over the years, is a monumental piece of hardware occupying most of an entire room. It consists primarily of two basic planes, motorized to move on x and y axes and motion controllable from the camera position to facilitate alignment of matte and painting elements. Although an aerial image system that would permit camera moves on the painting is in the works, the matte stand, as employed on *Blade Runner* — also *Close Encounters* and *Star Trek* — permitted only locked-off shots. Other features of the custom-built stand include a separate rear plane equipped with adjustable lighting elements that can be configured in various ways to burn glowing light sources into the painting or to provide a back-lighting medium for special effects enhancement.

"The matte camera runs in bipack," explained Richard Yuricich, chief architect of the system. "In the lower magazine we run an interpositive of the original stage photography. Then, raw duping stock — which will be our final effects negative — is loaded into the upper magazine so that during photography it runs down behind the interpositive. It's basically a two-pass system, although most of our matte shots require a good many more. The first pass is on the matte plane, which is clear glass covered with white paint that's been totally scraped away except for the areas of the frame where the original camera negative is to be retained. Behind the glass is a black velvet curtain. The matte glass is frontlit, so the white painted area becomes essentially a printing light for the camera. And since the negative stock is being run in bipack with the interpositive, only that portion of the frame which is aligned with the white matte area on the glass will print through. Then you wind the film back, and on the second pass you turn off the front lights on the matte glass, while in the second matte plane — which has its own lights — you position your painting. At the same time, you have to remember to remove the interpositive that's been running in bipack with the dupe negative, and replace it instead with a dummy reel of clear film so that the negative is still precisely the same distance away from the focal plane. Without its frontlighting, the white areas on the matte glass go to silhouette and act as a matte to protect the original negative that's already been exposed onto the dupe. Then you simply expose for the painting and the two are combined."

In practice, however, the process is rarely so simple. The average *Blade Runner* matte shot required a half-dozen in-camera passes, while one particularly elaborate one — eventually cut from the film — required twenty-three. "In a lot of ways," said assistant cameraman Robert Bailey, who was largely responsible for the matte photography, "Doug and Richard tend to use the matte stand like an optical printer. In *Blade Runner* we

Live-action elements featuring Harrison Ford and Edward James Olmos inside the flying spinner were photographed on a stage at The Burbank Studios. Months later, the cockpit mockup was transported to EEG where it was realigned to the camera in perfect registration with the earlier shot and positioned in front of a rear process screen. Miniature backgrounds could then be inserted into the scene while retaining natural canopy reflections and diffraction — embellished further by external rain and smoke effects. / The live-action setup at the studio featured its own rain and smoke effects, plus interactive lighting. / David Dryer lines up a point-of-view shot through the canopy. Interior vidscreen images were inserted optically and correlated closely with what was being seen outside.

CINEFEX 9 ▶ 45

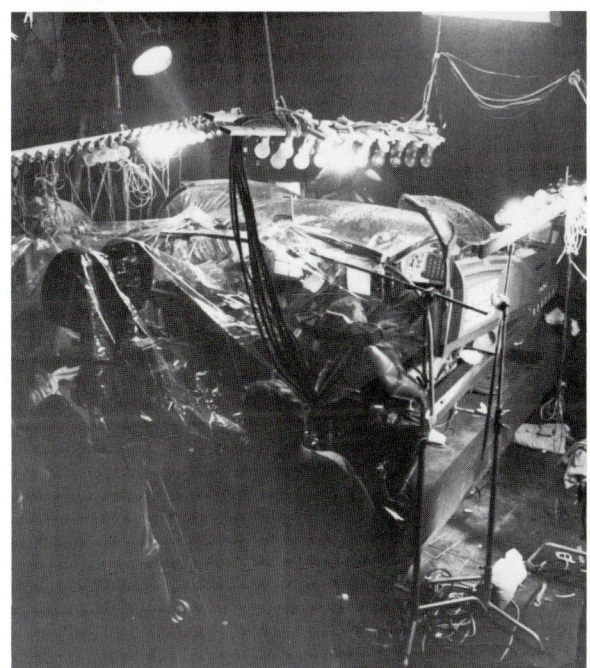

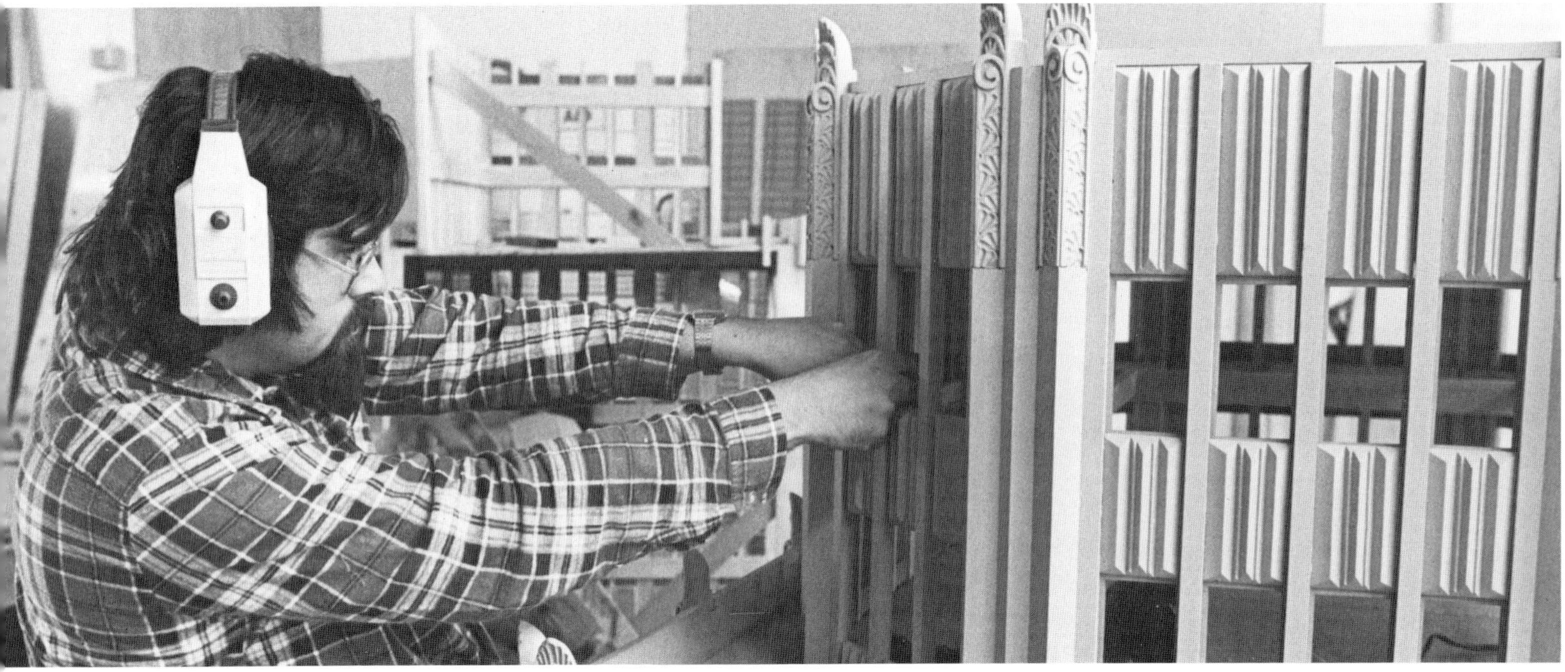

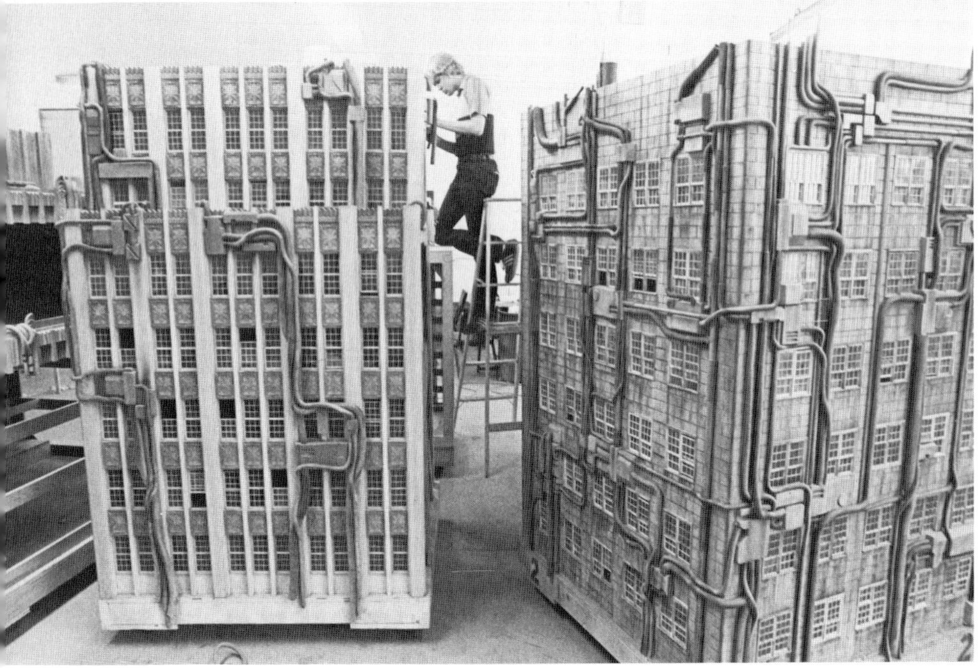

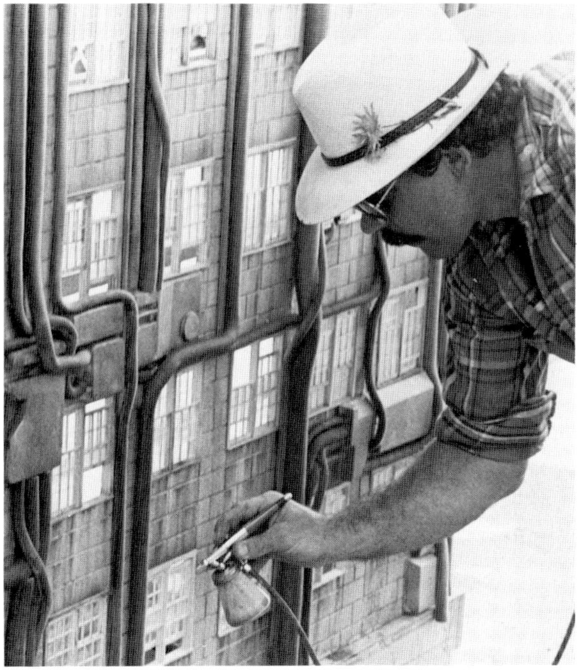

added rain and smoke and lightning flashes and a lot of other things you wouldn't necessarily expect from a matte stand. Of course, the prime consideration is always what will give the best effect, and in certain applications the matte stand has some very definite advantages. One of the real problems with opticals is that you can't start putting in a lot of optical elements without also starting to flash your highlights — particularly when you're trying to DX (double expose) photographic elements with thin or amorphous texture, such as rain and smoke. In these cases, a cover matte of normal density will create a very unconvincing burn-in — the smoke will have hard edges and the rain will appear too contrasty. To solve this, you have to either use a continuous tone stock, or very low exposures on a hi-con stock. In either case, there isn't sufficient matte density to prevent contaminating the overall scene. Sometimes that can work for you, because you want to desaturate the colors and kill the contrast — both of which are usually real good clues that you're looking at an optical effect. But a little goes a long way, and if you start putting in fifteen passes — as we did on some of those shots — you can just totally wash out everything. A lot of those elements, though, can be painted on a jet black shiny board and shot on the matte stand — and no matter how much light you pump onto it, you're not going to contaminate anything."

All other things considered, it is still the in-camera use of the 5243 duplicating stock — rather than the traditional 5247 color negative — that makes the EEG custom matting system most distinctive. It also produces some distinctive side effects. For one, since the stock is specifically intended for optical printer use — not in-camera use — the emulsion is much slower than color negative. "As a result," said Bailey, "it requires four to five thousand foot-candles for proper exposure — which is an incredible amount of light, and an incredible amount of electricity. But there's no question that when it comes to duplicating the process plates, you get a much better result if you can go on a duplicating stock rather than on an original camera stock." A less desirable characteristic, however — at least from the matte painter's perspective — is that while the duping stock records contrast and color accurately from a photographic point of view, it does *not* record them in the same way the human eye sees them. As a result, the painter has to paint to the stock rather than to the original negative stage photography.

Matthew Yuricich grumbles a lot about it, but not without unconcealed pride for the fact that only he and those he has trained have been able to cope with the exasperating unpredictability of the duping stock's response to color. "I really prefer painting on original negative. Who wouldn't? You paint what you see, and as an artist you can really go to your limits. With dupe stock you're never really sure. Nothing photographs the way it looks. Your darks are not very dark; and your lights have to be down because they'll pop up. And you can really end up with some garrish-looking colors. My brother insists on it because it holds a finer dupe and they're able to put all the other garbage in over it that they need. But sometimes I think the advantages of being able to hold a finer dupe turn out to be disadvantages in that the painting cannot be done as well — with all the feeling and guts and stuff that gives it life. I remember a long time ago talking to Peter Vlahos — who was head physicist, I believe, for the Motion Picture Research Council — about some problems I was having with 5253, which was the earlier-generation dupe stock we used up through *Close Encounters*. That stuff was *really* tough on the painter. Oftentimes you'd end up not being able to put all your abilities or talents into a painting because you'd be too busy trying to mentally transpose some crazy blotch of color — which may have been photographing just fine, but to the eye was making you sick. Anyway, I asked him something about it, and he said, 'You can't paint to it.' I said: 'What do you mean? I've been doing it for fifteen years!' Finally what he suggested was that I get Winsor Newton — whose paints I use — to give me the color spectrum analysis of the pigments, and then find the same thing as the colors in the shot, and then match this particular number to that particular number — and I said: 'Wait a minute! It'll take me a year to paint one shot!' Peter's solution was scientifically correct, but it didn't take into account aesthetics or practicability. So it really wasn't much help. It's been mainly just trial and error."

For Matthew Yuricich, the first step in producing a matte painting is to secure a clip from the live-action photography, which is then taken to the matte room, where the matte camera also doubles as a rotoscope projector. "The original negative is usually full-frame," said Bob Bailey. "There might be a flag in the shot sometimes to keep a light from flaring, but generally there won't be any in-front-of-camera mattes. This allows the greatest amount of flexibility in where to put the matte line later on. We put the clip in and project it up onto a white board. Matthew then decides where he wants the matte line to be and he'll draw a line. We'll make a countermatte by blackening in the area on the board which will correspond to the area the painting will occupy on the painting board. Then we'll shoot a hi-con matte which will give us the area we want to burn out — which is literally what we do. When optical makes the interpositive, they transfer the negative intact to the IP stock. Then, while it's still latent, they'll go back and use this matte that we've made to just burn white light in — to burn out, or blacken, the area where the painting's going to go. That's necessary because one of the problems early effects people using dupe stock found was that external mattes used in normal matte shots weren't black enough on the IP image to keep the painting area from being flashed when the dupe negative was made. That's why the matte area on the latent IP is burned out first. Then it's sent to the lab and processed, and we now have an IP that has the live-action on it — with the area we want the painting in, black.

"Sometimes we didn't use the IP technique — but not often. There's one scene at the end where Harrison Ford is hanging from the side of a building and about to fall, and Rutger Hauer jumps across from one building to the other, right over his head. That was duplicated on the optical printer with a low-density

The first phase of the cityscape was designed by Wayne Smith, who initiated construction of a dozen buildings ranging from quarter-inch to one-inch scale — some of which had completely furnished interiors. Construction foreman Jerry Allen works on one of the art deco facades. / Jon Roennau adds upper story detailing to one at the tallest structures. Since the effects budget was limited, the intent was to build a small number of versatile two- and three-sided structures which could be rearranged and redressed for use in various places throughout the film. / Ron Gress applies an airbrushed aging solution to one of the completed miniatures. The initial cityscape was completed in record time, but many of the larger structures were to see only limited use when a last-minute decision was made to decrease the overall scale.

cover matte and then brought latent to the matte painting room where we added the painting in much the same way as you would on original negative. The live-action area on the painting would be painted black, and we'd have to do little move tests on it in a variety of directions — east, west, north and south — and then take those pieces of footage and process them in a little black-and-white hand tank until we were sure we had it lined up right and we weren't getting a matte line. With our other technique, it's impossible to get a matte line, because your duping glass is the same one you use for the matte — so it *has* to fit."

Even before the duping stage, however, a color-corrected clip from the live-action daily was given to Virgil Mirano who used it to produce a twenty-inch-wide color positive print, which was given in turn to Syd Mead whose duties had been expanded to designing the matte shots. Working closely with Ridley Scott, Mead painted his extended visions directly over the screen-proportioned color prints. "The design flavor of the film was, of course, already established," said Mead, "so that philosophy was already incorporated into the set construction. My job was to extend that by adding more detail and maintaining the same technological retrofitted look throughout the city. It was really a lot of fun, like painting huge machines off in the distance. But the film approach took some getting used to. I've done rendering all my professional life — twenty some years — but the particular things you have to do to make it work on film were new to me. You have to deal with forced perspective and lens perspective and maybe three different vanishing points all going in different directions on the perspective grid. You'd never get away with those things in an architectural rendering, because everything's so distorted. But that's what was needed here, so I learned from talking with Matt and Richard Yuricich what you can and cannot do to make something come off on film. One of the things we had to do was try and disguise the matte line by interweaving the painted image with the real so that you didn't get an obvious crossover between the real set and matte painting. Some of the sets, for instance, had cables running up the side of a building. Well, if you run a cable across a matte line like that — where there's lots of specific detail — it has to be absolutely perfect. If there's even the slightest little bit of jiggle in the multiple exposures, you can see it right away. So when they built the set, they would have an accumulation of transformers and cables that would all collect at the top of the set, and then I would invent an intermediate row in the painting — in some cases where another line of cables would collect at a transformer just above that — so your eye would go from large detail block to large detail block and then continue on; and you'd forget about the fact that there might be a matte line. It's sort of a mental camouflage system that you can use."

"Ridley and Syd worked together very closely on the matte designs," said Matthew Yuricich. "Syd would get these enlargements and talk with Ridley about what he wanted, and then he'd disappear for a while. When he came back with what he thought Ridley wanted, the two of them would get together again and

Effects supervisor David Dryer and cameraman John Seay prepare for one of the cityscape shots. / Pat Van Auken, John Seay and David Hardberger align a process projector used to cast advertising messages onto an off-camera video billboard. / Spinner passages through the cityscape provide the film with some of its most breathtaking moments. Flying vehicles were recorded as separate film elements, as were the gigantic billboard images. / Leon's hotel as constructed in miniature. Circular dental mirrors were used to throw small pools of reflected light into designated areas. / David Dryer studies one of the setups.

CINEFEX 9 ▶ 49

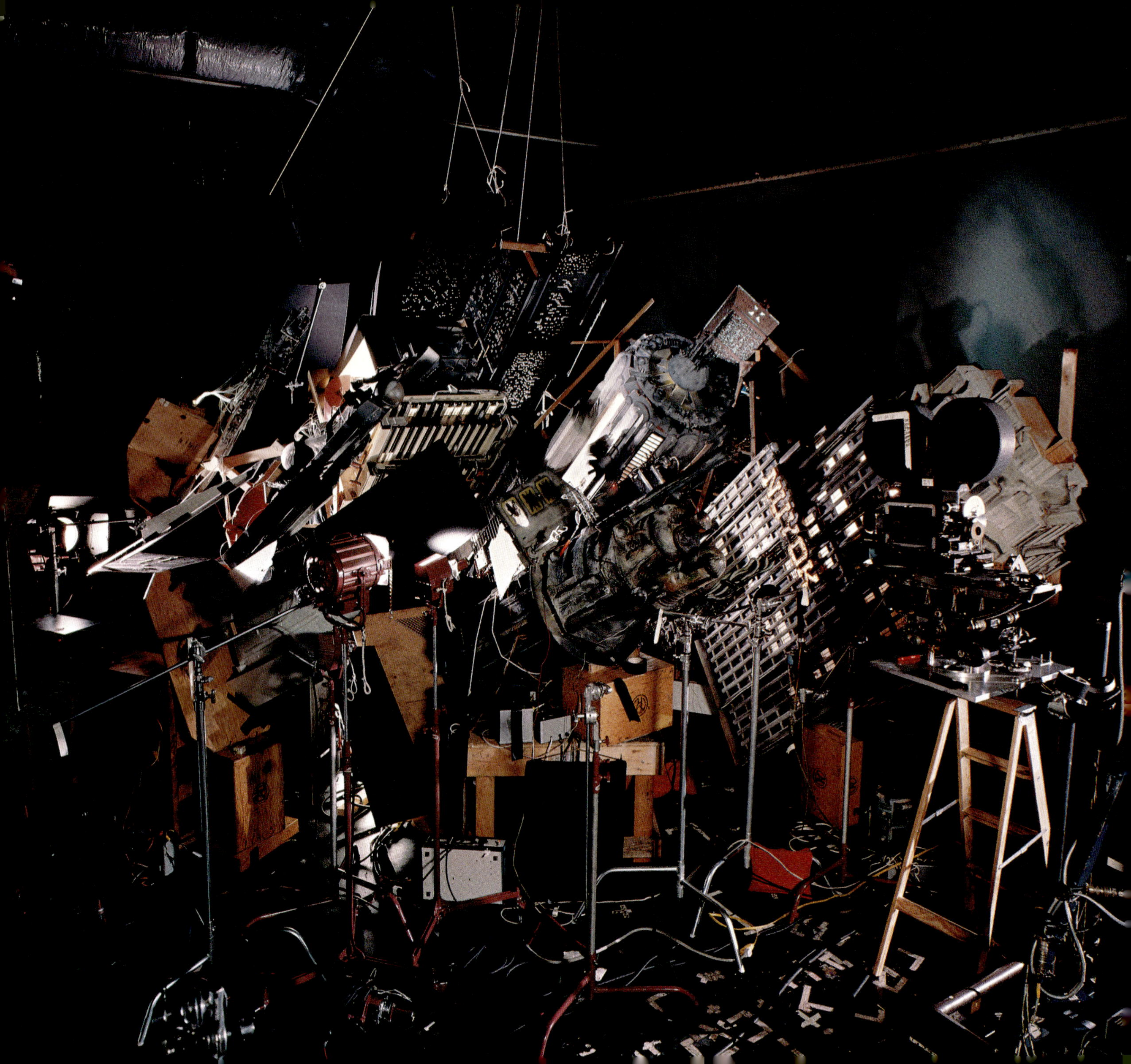

Ridley would say, 'No, I'd like this changed or that.' And Syd would disappear back to his place again and rework it. So by the time it got to me, it was *exactly* what Ridley wanted — right down to the last pipe. Which is fine with me. I'd much rather have that than somebody who doesn't know *what* he wants. My big bitch — and everybody I've worked with is tired of hearing me say it — but to me there's nothing worse than to be sitting in the screening room after you've painted something and have the director or somebody say, 'Well, I think this building should be over here on the right.' And I'll say, 'Why the hell didn't you change it on the sketch — on the illustration?! That's what it's for!' You work and you paint and that's fine. But to change it, that's labor. It's like something you've already done, and it's ten times harder to get into that than it is when you're starting fresh on something and waiting with anticipation to see how it's going to come out. The same creative juices just aren't there. So I was very happy to get what I got on *Blade Runner*. Most of the time when I do matte shots for other people, I have to do a lot of design and research myself. If I'm lucky, I'll get a very crude pencil sketch. Syd's illustrations were definitely the best I've ever had to work from. All I had to do was transfer the whole idea. But since Ridley was so particular about reproducing them exactly, we started out spending half our time just trying to trace the sketch. We'd photograph it and project it on a board and trace it out and draw it in, and try to save as much of the stuff he wanted as possible.''

Matthew Yuricich had always lamented the fact that, on the EEG matte stand designed by his brother, he was never able to paint directly onto photographic enlargements as he had done regularly over the years on such diverse projects as *Ben-Hur* and *Logan's Run*. The problem sprang primarily from the extreme slowness of the duplicating film stock — though it did not manifest itself particularly with the old Clarence Slifer system, which compensated by using about a five-second exposure per frame. Richard Yuricich, however, felt that such lengthy exposures were a major drawback to the technique, and that the time required to complete a multi-pass matte shot would diminish the system's overall effectiveness. To compensate, he increased the amount of light — drastically.

"I can only speak in superlatives about the intensity of the light on that matte stand," said Virgil Mirano. "It's just extraordinary. There are four banks of thousand-watt quartz lights, and each bank has eight to ten lights. So the amount of light is *immense* — but so is the amount of heat. At M·G·M, Matthew Yuricich had matte boards coated with photographic emulsion, projected an image onto them, developed them, and then painted directly over that. At EEG, however, there was a problem in trying to rediscover that technology, because the heat generated on the matte stand was so intense that it would melt, flake or distort standard photographic papers. Or if you put on a coated emulsion, it would peel it right off. The problem with the current generation of photographic papers is that they are resin-coated; and large-scale, resin-coated papers tend to be extremely difficult to mount. I thought if I could find a non-resin-based, photosensitive paper and have it mounted in the proper fashion, it would probably work.''

Finding the proper paper — even in black-and-white — was no easy task, particularly since the masonite matte boards to be covered measured seven feet long by three feet high. Once he did, though, Mirano farmed the project out to a firm that specialized in flawless photographic mounting, and the end result did indeed withstand the ravages of the scorching matte stand. With proper care and alignment, monochrome versions of Syd Mead's renderings could thus be applied in perfect registration, directly to the matte boards, thereby saving hours of tedious hand-tracing. Once that was done, the painting could proceed in the usual manner.

"The enlargements were great," said Yuricich. "If we'd started with them from the beginning, we'd have probably finished three months earlier. But one thing about working with them is that even though you might match your colors by eye to the colors you want, they photograph differently — because most of the time the paper burns right on through, even when it's covered with paint. Especially the black-and-white, which is actually kind of reddish. So if I need green foliage, for example — and I'm using a black-and-white enlargement — I have to use poison green, which balances with the red light coming through from the enlargement and changes the color to what I really want. It's no big deal, but it's one of the things you have to learn as you work with it. For the most part, we had to paint over the enlargements completely, just to match the colors in the dupe. But in some places, the enlargement held up so well in certain sections that we could just glaze over it and retain the drawing from underneath.''

In all, about fifteen full-blown matte paintings were produced for *Blade Runner*, plus numerous partial paintings and miscellaneous patch-up jobs. A half dozen of the major paintings appear in the early sections of the film to open it up and show a wider view of the teeming megalopolis. Their most dramatic use, however, was in the climactic rooftop chase between Deckard and the replicant ringleader, Roy Batty, where fully nine of the paintings were employed to create a vertiginous sense of scale and perspective. "Originally, the plan was not to use matte paintings," Richard Yuricich revealed. "Instead, they were going to shoot in downtown Los Angeles with stuntmen, and then use small set pieces on a stage with front projection for the scenes where you can really tell it's Harrison Ford and Rutger Hauer. But getting the front projection plates ready in time would have been a problem; and the downtown shooting would have been dangerous. So we suggested going with matte paintings instead, and that's what they decided to do. Larry Paull and his art director, Dave Snyder, built some very clever partial sets on the backlot, and those were used for the entire sequence.'' From the start, it had been intended that the chase sequence paintings would be done on original negative — primarily as a time and cost-saving measure — and indeed the main unit photography was shot with that in mind, using external mattes

In order to get aerial views of some of the cityscapes, the miniature structures — many of them short-notice requirements created from scratch in hours — were tilted sideways and aligned individually at varying angles so as to appear correct to the barrel distortion of the camera's wide-angle lens. As always, numerous in-camera passes were required to balance external and practical lighting. Separate multi-pass film elements were also created for the various billboard and spinner insertions. Like most of the other miniature work, the cityscapes were filmed in smoke and augmented optically with rain.

A smoke room pass on one of the aerial cityscape scenes. / Matte elements were generated by placing evenly-lit white cards behind the miniature setups — which themselves were left unlit — thereby creating a silhouette matte as the camera cycled through a repeat of its motion control move. The spindly, wedge-shaped building in the center is Bill George's extensively embellished replica of the Millennium Falcon. / One of the most difficult shots in the film was a traveling aerial view of the city as a spinner spirals down to land on the roof of the police precinct tower. Even the most complex curving moves were achieved solely through simple straight-line trajectories.

to isolate the live-action elements. However, Ridley Scott's increased employment of rain and smoke throughout the production ultimately caused Richard Yuricich to consider the approach too chancy, and so he changed direction and opted instead to go with their normal dupe negative technique.

At best, though, the normal technique was a time-consuming one, and from start to finish Matthew Yuricich wound up devoting nine months to the *Blade Runner* project. An early attempt had been made to secure the added services of Rocco Gioffre — who, under Yuricich's tutelage, had blossomed into a fine matte painter in his own right — but Gioffre and five other young alumni from the Trumbull organization had started their own effects firm after *Star Trek*, and at the time he was committed to other projects. Although Yuricich had taken on a new apprentice, Michelle Moen, she was only beginning to learn the complexities of the craft and was spending much of her time producing mattes and special effects gags for the paintings. When Gioffre's schedule finally opened up, he was added to the *Blade Runner* crew.

Painting in the evenings, with the same easel and equipment used by Yuricich during the day, Gioffre spent about three months working on basically four extensive matte paintings. His first was a high-angle view of Sean Young crossing a rubbish-cluttered intersection on foot. Shot from a rooftop in downtown Los Angeles, the actual street setting had been dressed with futuristic props and vehicles, and as conceived was to have been augmented with matte-painted cutout areas revealing glimpses of a high-speed, multilayered freeway system below the basic real-world street level. The shot had been completed earlier in the show by Matthew Yuricich — and had been approved. Weeks later, however, Ridley Scott began having second thoughts about the design concept, which in retrospect seemed unclear. "In discussing what was wrong with the shot," Matthew Yuricich commented, "I suggested elimination of one underpass — which was superfluous and busy — plus changing to a warm brownish color since the existing streets were cool and dark. Also I thought that to really sell the underpass, cars or spinners should be put in for realism and movement." By the time a final decision was made to redo the shot, Yuricich was deeply engrossed in several other paintings, and so the job was relegated to Rocco Gioffre, who at that point had just come on the project.

"What started out as a few alterations," said Gioffre, "ended up being pretty much an entire repaint of the underpasses, because they decided they wanted to change levels around and fool with the lighting a bit and make it look a little more wet. They started to opt toward really soggy-looking matte paintings about halfway into the show, so they'd intercut better with the closeups where it's pouring rain. As a result, we had to start working more on reflections on the road and that sort of thing. But the main problem with the shot was the underpasses. They didn't especially look like they were underneath the real intersection, or that they went down a couple levels. So the shot was simplified by removing one of the freeway underpasses and changing the direction of another one slightly. The lighting was also changed. It was formerly darker down below, and they changed it so it was actually brighter than the foreground stuff." Once his first assignment was completed, Gioffre went on to paint two others in the final chase sequence, and then started a third which was later finished by Yuricich.

Perfecting a matte painting is rarely a simple or speedy matter — even under the most ideal of circumstances — but the process tends to be even more arduous and convoluted when duplicate film stock enters the equation. "In lots of cases," Gioffre explained, "seven or eight — or even nine — different painting tests will have to be shot on the matte stand before we get it just right. The way we start is that once the sketch for the lay-in stage of the matte painting is done — in other words, the first paint is put on the board — the painting is taken to the matte camera for testing against an interpositive dupe of the live-action. Of course, the first test has the widest and most variety of colors and densities, so they can find out if we're in the ballpark. Usually the paintings are off by a mile. But at that point you can usually nail down what color filter they are going to use in front of the matte painting — whether it's a slight cyan correction or slight magenta, and the only wedge testing that'll be done over that will be an exposure density wedge which will show the painting from too light to too dark against a fixed exposure of the live-action. Then it's a matter of repainting and trying to match the colors, and wedge-testing it again on the matte stand. At this point, it should be a little bit closer — hopefully not any farther away, although that sometimes happens because it's hard to estimate the corrections you need to paint with the duping stock. It just takes a little more testing and time. You're not going to hit the colors and contrasts as easily as you would with regular Eastman color negative, where you can paint black and *see* black and where your contrast is pretty much the way your eye sees it. With the duping stock, you have to develop an eye for low contrast and muted colors. So we keep repainting and rephotographing; and that will go on day after day, for several weeks sometimes — especially on this project, because there were so many other elements going into the composites that sometimes we'd need to go back in and compensate for contamination or something. But generally, within a week or two, we could usually get our colors and densities to match the colors and densities on the live-action."

Matthew Yuricich offered a somewhat more cynical perspective on how long it takes to complete a matte shot. "Lots of times I'll do something, and I don't like it and I don't think it's ready. But it's near the end of the picture and the pressure's on — like *Star Trek* — and all of a sudden the paintings start looking real great after the first hour. And that would be after others that I'd put three months in on that weren't *ever* quite good enough. Years ago at M-G-M, I used to paint big suns or moons in them — something that looked perfectly terrible, but could be painted out easily — just so they couldn't take them away from me until I thought they were finished. The *Blade Runner* paintings weren't

CINEFEX 9 ▶ 53

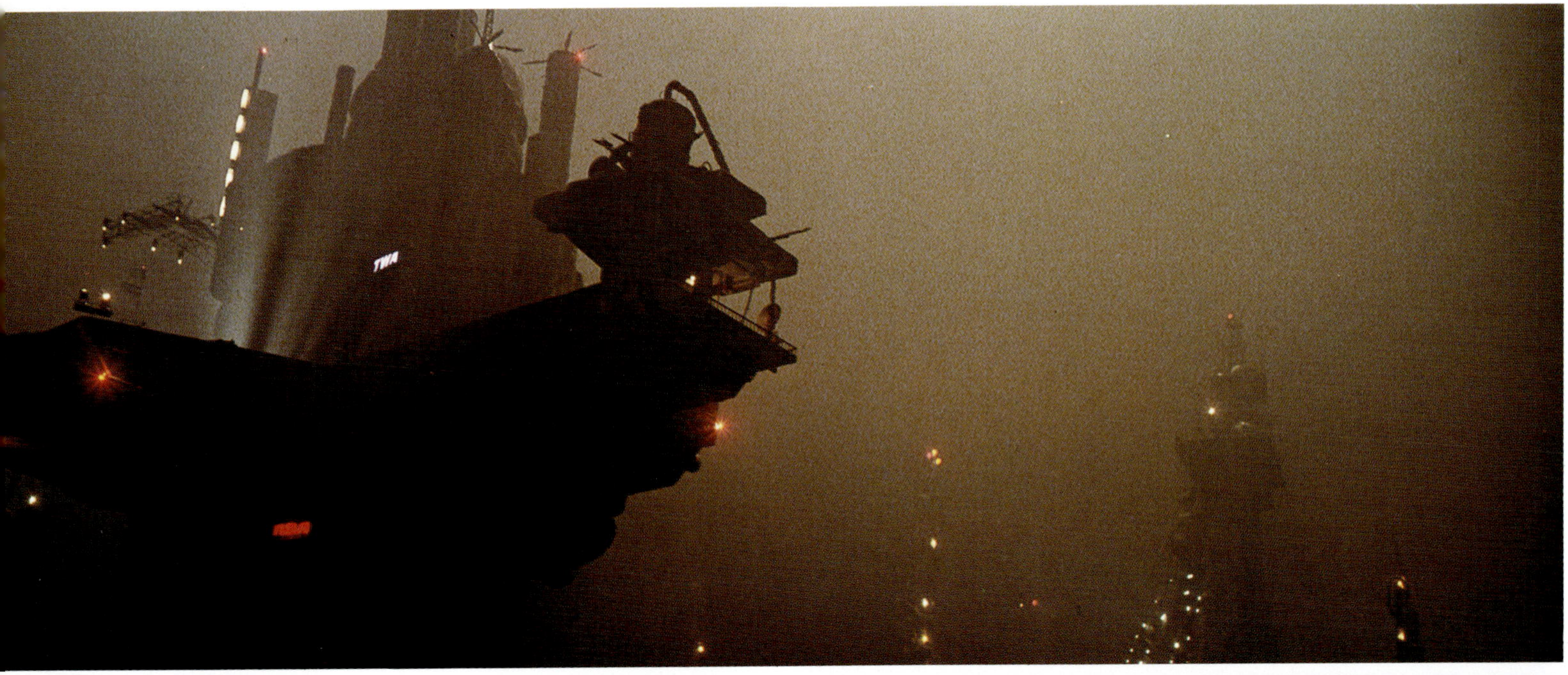
TWA

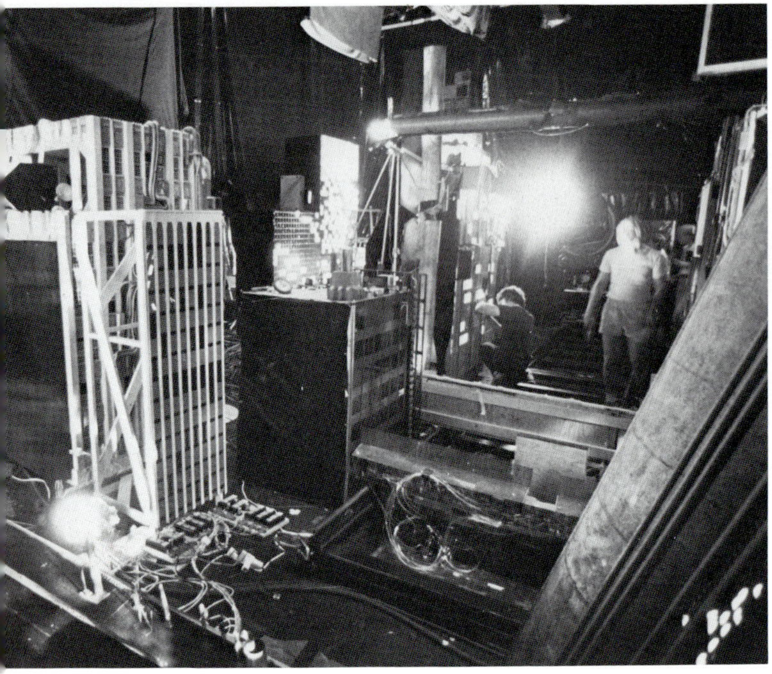

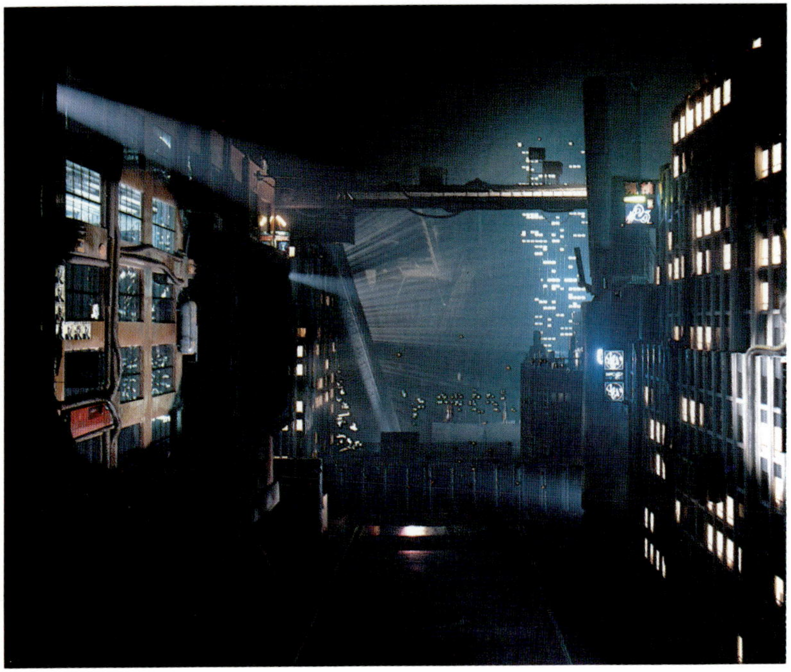

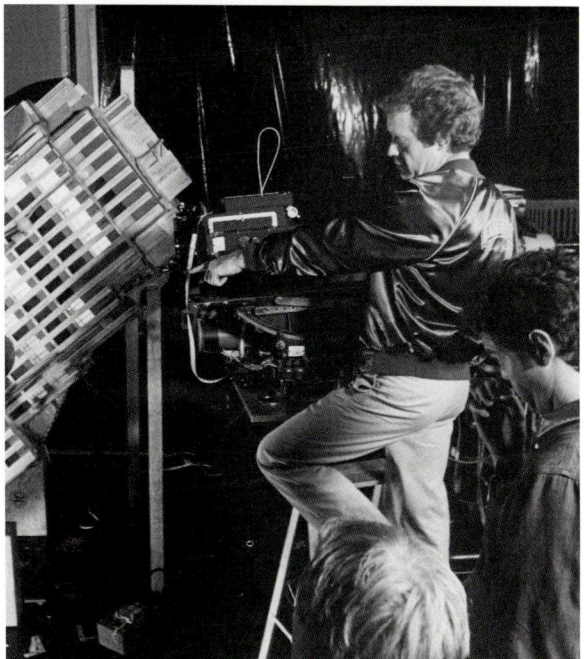

particularly hard to paint, but they *were* hard to make credible. One of the things about matte shots is that if you have buildings or trees or anything else that's *real* in the original, you try to carry that same flavor over into the painting. It kind of ties it all together. The tough part about *Blade Runner* was that there were all these standard old buildings that everyone's used to; and then, all of a sudden, you have this futuristic-looking stuff looming right up behind. And it's difficult trying to make those two elements fit together. A really good matte shot you'll never know, as long as the painting fits in with what's around it. When you're working with the future, though, and you're painting something the audience *knows* has to be fake, the job is just doubly difficult trying to make it work."

What really sets the *Blade Runner* matte paintings apart from most others, however, is the extent to which they have been treated as dimensional entities. Puddles of painted water shimmer with reflected neon; streams of traffic jockey for position on distant painted causeways; spinners soar into frame, only to disappear behind a painted building and emerge again on the other side. None of these things are exactly revolutionary, but the sheer virtuosity with which two- and three-dimensional subjects are blended together represents what is probably the most bravura use of matte paintings in years — perhaps ever.

One of the flashiest techniques employed was to insert traveling matte miniature elements — usually spinners — into the shots. A relatively simple way of doing this would be to treat the completed matte shot as a background plate and run it through the optical printer with the necessary mattes and countermattes required for adding the disparate spinner element photographed on the effects stages. But to do so would take the final composite another generation away from original photography. Avoiding that extra generation — and its attendant loss of image quality — involved employing a variation of the basic matte photography technique first devised by Richard Yuricich for *Close Encounters of the Third Kind*. "The first step is to put the live-action portion of the scene onto the dupe negative, using the burned-out interpositive that we'd normally be running in bipack on the matte stand. For a traveling matte shot though, obviously we need a traveling matte — and since there's no room in the matte camera for a third piece of film, we get around that by doing our first duping step in the optical printer. So now we have the live-action portion of the shot on the dupe negative, with the painting area still unexposed. That negative is held latent and taken to the matte stand. Since the live-action has already been exposed, there's no need to run the IP on the matte stand. Instead, we bipack the traveling matte of the miniature — or whatever else it may be — to the dupe negative and run them together for the painting pass. We now have the painting and the live-action combined, but with the traveling matte area still unexposed. The negative is then taken — still undeveloped — back to the optical printer, where it's run with a complementary cover matte to insert the traveling matte elements."

Though less common, in one instance — for a dizzying down-

A towering pit stop — dubbed the Sushi Tower by the effects crew — was created as an insert for the Hades overflight. The distinctive structure was redressed several times, however, and found its way into numerous cityscape scenes as well. / The stage crew setting up for a point-of-view shot which will later be projected through the spinner canopy. / A reverse angle of the final setup. In addition to the miniature structures, a rear-projected Syd Mead painting was used in the very back. / Model shop supervisor Mark Stetson adds last-minute refinements to the Sushi Tower. / Once principal photography was completed, Ridley Scott shifted his attention to the effects effort, closely supervising every aspect of the postproduction work.

Working from a design concept provided by Syd Mead, artist Matthew Yuricich roughs in a matte painting for the scene in which Deckard strolls out on his balcony and gazes absently at the teeming megalopolis below. / Matte cameraman Robert Bailey prepares a moire pattern slot gag on the front plane of the matte stand. / The historic Bradbury Building in downtown Los Angeles provided the setting for Sebastian's apartment. From the original, live-action production take, an interpositive is generated, with a burned-out section corresponding to the area the painting would later occupy. The interpositive is then run in bipack with raw dupe negative stock as the painting goes through a series of wedge tests and refinements until it blends perfectly with the live-action photography. Once painting and live-action are combined, other effects can be added. In this case, Michelle Moen and Bob Bailey align a matte board which will be photographed and superimposed over the painting to boost the light level coming from the street lights.

angle shot in which Deckard is clinging desparately by his nails from the roof of a skyscraper — a traveling matte was required to insert Harrison Ford into the scene, since the composition of the shot required that his feet dangle directly over the painted city street hundreds of feet below. Like the rest of the sequence, the shot was filmed on The Burbank Studios backlot, using a mockup rooftop that was in reality only about twelve feet off the ground and skirted with cushioned airbags. During photography, a large white card was positioned beneath the actor to help differentiate his body more clearly from the background. The live-action was then rotoscoped on the matte stand so a split screen could be drawn along the foreground edge of the building, and the area above — not already isolated by the white backdrop — garbage-matted out. From there, a cover matte was generated to isolate the Harrison Ford portion of the live-action onto a dupe negative, which was then run latent with the corresponding holdout matte during photography of the painting.

Numerous other techniques, usually involving in-camera passes on the matte stand and/or latent passes through the optical printer, were used to enhance the matte shots, but at the same time avoid "double-duping" — a virtual taboo at EEG. Among the most troublesome insertions was the addition of rain and smoke elements into nearly all of the shots. Although it had not originally been anticipated, the rain-drenched sogginess which came to permeate the live-action photography soon spilled over into the effects. "The whole film takes place over a period of about three days," Ridley Scott explained. "And like all good sort of Philip Marlowe-type stories, it seems always to be at night. The rain just kind of made things more interesting. Except for one scene, the entire film was done on the studio backlot; and backlot streets just work better when they're wet and at night — especially with all the neon and advertising that we had. Any way you look at it, ten thousand people going up and down the street in pouring rain with umbrellas up is a helluva lot more interesting to look at than a dry old backlot street." As always, any shot requiring postproduction optical work was filmed in 65mm, with either Douglas Trumbull or Richard Yuricich — or later David Dryer — routinely on hand to supervise the setup and provide technical expertise. "The first time that rain and smoke came up in a matte shot," Yuricich recalled, "was when Ridley Scott sweet-talked us — me, actually — into doing it. So to cover ourselves, we shot a take with, and one without. But as he got further into the production, Ridley — being extremely artistic and very, very demanding — started shooting *everything* in the rain. So at that point, we really had no choice. We had to come up with some way of dealing with it — and we're glad Ridley insisted."

The most pressing problem was how to deal with rain and smoke, and occasionally light beams, crossing over matte lines. To afford themselves the most coverage and protection, such shots were usually photographed with and without the troublesome elements, and frequently with varying amounts to see how much they could actually get away with. Obviously,

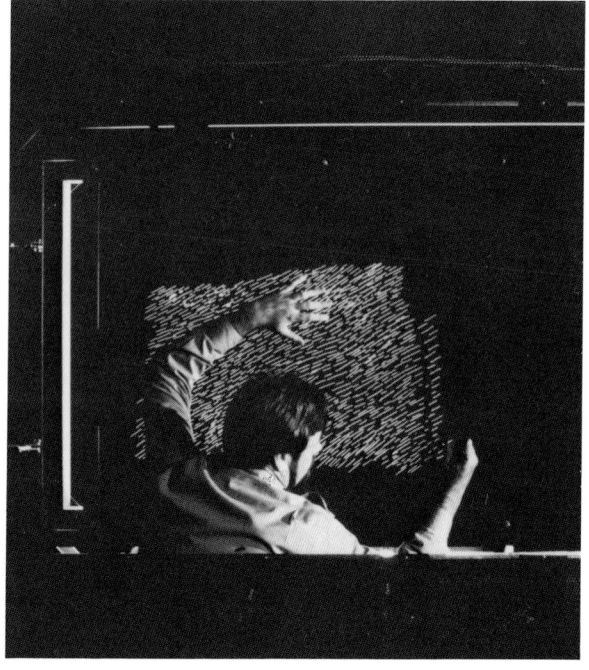

CINEFEX 9 ▶ 57

58 ◀ CINEFEX 9

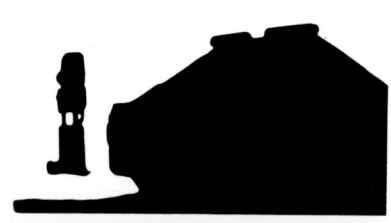

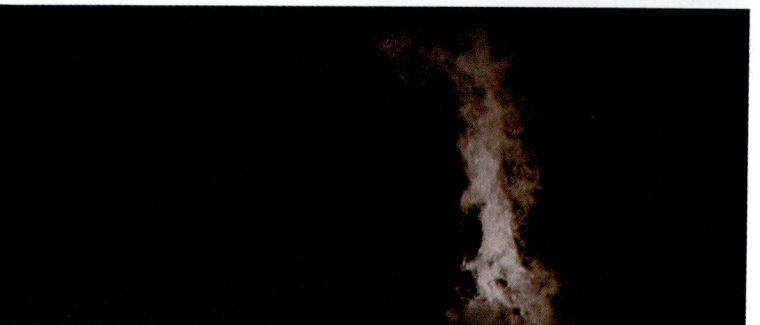

however, additional rain and smoke elements would have to be generated to composite into both miniature setups and painted areas. This necessitated another late-night foray into the EEG parking lot. Lights and cameras were set up. A number of hoses were dragged up onto the roof, and for about three hours the crew shot a whole range of simulated rain effects — from heavy downpours to light misting. From there it was a matter of making black-and-white prints that could be superimposed in over the dry effects footage.

Although the optical department added rain to most of the miniature shots, much of the matte painting embellishment was done on the matte stand. "It's *really* tough to put rain in after the fact and make it look right," said Bob Bailey, "On some of the early shots, the rain was just double-exposed over the composited painting and live-action — and it *looked* double-exposed, like a curtain hanging in front of the shot. We didn't do any of the obvious idiocies like you used to see in some older films, where the scene would pan but the rain wouldn't. But it was still hard to make it look realistic. We studied a lot of rain footage, and after a while we realized that at night you really only see rain falling in an area where there's a light source. So we decided to make a black-and-white print off a previous composite and then put the rain in — not overall, but burn it through that black-and-white so that only the bright areas, the highlight areas, would have rain, and the rest of it would stay dark. That looked very realistic. And it gave the shot depth, because the rain seemed to be appearing only where it would naturally and didn't look like it was just put in over the whole thing."

A number of other matte stand tricks — many of them near-subliminal — were used to add extra dimension to the *Blade Runner* shots. "Oftentimes you'll see matte paintings with *some* gags in them," said Rocco Gioffre, "but on this particular show, there were a *huge* number of additional effects that went in on top of the paintings. Michelle Moen was primarily responsible for the creation of the art that went into the gags that were done on the matte stand, but I did a few as well. A lot of them were just different basic slot gags — or moire patterns — that would be used to create little rippling effects and street reflections in the painted water. That entailed putting colored gels, which matched the neon signs in the painting, behind a piece of glass that was opaque, but with scratched areas on it. That was backlit from behind the matte stand with little slide projector-type lamps aimed directly at the camera lens. Then, in the front plane of the matte stand there'd be an interference pattern that would be either diagonal lines or wavy diagonal lines — something of that nature — that would break up the scratches that were stationary in the back plane and create kind of a rippling effect that would be double-exposed over the painting on a separate pass. Sometimes there were a couple of different passes so that the rippling wasn't all going at one speed. Some would catch up and others would pass, and you could get a little bit of overlapping double exposure to create the illusion of the water moving in the street down below."

Other gags were not so conventional. The live-action portion of the high-angle down-shot on which both Yuricich and Gioffre painted was originally determined to be too bright overall, and so the shot was printed down to the desired level of illumination. In doing so, however, the key element of the shot — Rachael crossing the intersection — virtually disappeared into the shadows. The solution to the problem was one that Matthew Yuricich had carried in his bag of tricks since *Forbidden Planet* when a similar situation arose in a matte shot for the sequence in which Morbius and his unwelcome guests are touring the vast Krell underground. In that instance, by taking a black matte board and painting some white concentric circles on it, Yuricich had been able to create an artificial pool of light which was then superimposed over the shot in such a way as to draw attention to the minute human figures which had previously been all but indiscernible. In studying the troublesome *Blade Runner* shot, Yuricich discovered a light standard in the general vicinity of Rachael's passage. "A clip from the live-action was taken," said Bob Bailey, "and rotoscoped on the matte stand. Then Matthew took a black board and stippled some white paint around the area where the girl walks through. Then, when the duplicate was made, we burned that white area in over it, which tended to act as a selective flash and make the overall exposure come up in that specific area. So what it looked like was a little pool of light, and she walks right through it. We used the same basic technique for a lot of the rain that was put in on the matte stand. We'd take black boards with soft white painted areas corresponding to lights in the shot — or coming from behind buildings and things, where you'd expect there to be light. In one case, we even painted in a searchlight. Then we'd bipack the overall black-and-white rain footage with our latent composite, and just shoot these flash boards which would make the rain show up in whatever areas we'd selected. The one scene of Harrison Ford hanging from his fingertips was especially interesting. The camera was looking straight down at the street and there weren't any obvious areas of light to illuminate the rain. But the overall rain effect — which was specially shot in a down-angle for this scene — just wasn't working. So we ended up using *two* different boards — with a couple of strange camouflage-like patterns on them — and we'd cycle those and dissolve back and forth between them. And what it did was make it look as though the rain was coming down and sort of swirling around in gusts. It was very effective.

"A lot of these kinds of things, you *could* do on an optical printer, but what's really nice about the matte stand is that you're working on a really huge expanse and you can be very, very selective in the areas you want to make brighter — or darker. On a lot of our composites we did things like selectively darken areas on our duping plane to kill highlights that were objectionable. On one in particular, the side of a duped building wasn't matching the rest of the 35mm live-action. At the exposure that was right for everything else, this one building was just too yellow. It looked like sandstone. So we ended up painting the highlight areas on the duping glass blue, which sub-

The Blade Runner *matte paintings featured unusually extensive special effects, as indicated by the annotated frame enlargement from the preliminary matte composite (bottom left) showing areas where effects were to be added. Rain and smoke — two elements generally avoided in matte paintings — were used extensively. In this case, a matte was derived from the vehicle on the right so that smoke could be made to appear as though it were coming from behind it. Not all matte painting effects were done on the matte stand. The sweeping spotlight was filmed in the smoke room and optically superimposed over the latent matte shot.*

tracted out the yellow light and gave us a gray building like the rest of them. To do something like that on an optical printer would be almost impossible. One thing about working with the 5243 stock, though, is that it's difficult to achieve some of the effects that are fairly easy if you're working with 5247. Things like lightning can usually be done on 5247 with just one pass, using a fog filter or some other kind of diffusion. With 5243, you usually need two passes — one for the bright element that's sharp and clear, and another for the glow. The stuff is just so miserably slow that your usual bag-of-tricks filters — all the scratch filters and star filters and diffusion and fog — just don't work very well."

Once principal photography wrapped, Ridley Scott became a pervasive figure around EEG — totally absorbed in every frame of film being produced for his picture. "Ridley's visual style is very special and very specific," David Dryer commented. "He has a very definite idea of the look and the feeling and the texture that he wants, and a degree here or a degree there is very important to him. Our job, as I saw it, was to open up the film and give it more scale — to give it a setting and take it out of the realm of the traditional, claustrophobic police drama, which is really what it is. And of course, we wanted the effects to work in support of the story, as well. All this in the context of Ridley's vision — which may not be the definitive future, but it's certainly a good possibility. So our assignment was not only to produce good-looking, believable effects, but also to match the texture and the feeling of the live-action, which had a lot of smoke and a lot of rain and a lot of other things that make effects work very difficult. And Ridley was very involved all the way through — lining up shots and giving suggestions. Sometimes we'd all wish we were on our own; but in all honesty, I must say he helped the shots a lot. He's got a terrific eye. And it was *his* film, so it was our job to give him exactly what he wanted."

Getting exactly what he wanted in the way of effects was an unaccustomed pleasure for Ridley Scott. "We did *Alien* at Bray Studios," he explained, "which had none of the technical capabilities that they have here, or the experience that they have here. So all the effects on *Alien* were very basic and very much rule-of-thumb. We would do one, stare at it, think 'Jesus, that doesn't work,' and then either accept it or go back to the drawing board and start again. So I was very limited in what I could actually do. This place is an altogether different kind of environment. It's like a laboratory where your failures are fewer because the technical capabilities are here and everybody is so experienced that you avoid all sorts of pitfalls. Whatever I came up with, they were able to produce — if not exactly, at least in some form or other. It was a real revelation."

As Ridley Scott became more and more engrossed in postproduction, he began pressing for additional effects scenes to expand his vision. Since every expenditure over and above the original budget had to be approved by the *Blade Runner* company, auditor Diana Gold — who had been hired by the producers as a combination effects production manager and financial liaison — was to become very much involved in the piecemeal

The climactic rooftop chase between Deckard and Batty featured extensive use of matte paintings. Partial sets were constructed on The Burbank Studios backlot so Harrison Ford and Rutger Hauer could perform in relative safety. / A Matthew Yuricich matte painting transformed the actual six-foot drop into a forty-story nightmare. / When Deckard rounds the corner, another dizzying view was painted by Rocco Gioffre.

CINEFEX 9 ▶ 61

62 ◀ CINEFEX 9

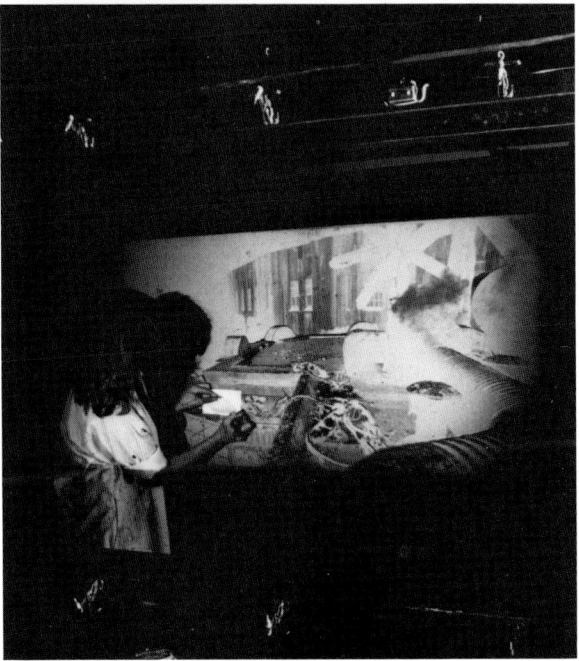

expansion process. "Every single shot would have to be budgeted down to the dollar, which was very laborious. Then each one had to be submitted to the producer and the financial people and they would decide at that point whether to proceed or not. Ridley Scott — being very persuasive — would put in his plea; and nine times out of ten, he got what he wanted."

"I think as Ridley got deeper into the film," said Dryer, "as *everybody* got deeper into it — they began to see the need for more and more effects shots to open it up and establish where they were and what was really going on. And they've pulled no punches. When a flying car's supposed to come down the street, a flying car *comes* down the street. It isn't done by suggestion — we actually cut to it and you see it happen. And in many cases, we're throwing away effects. This is certainly not new in effects films, but we went to a lot of trouble to put something together sometimes so as *not* to make the most out of the effect. The whole traffic sequence, for example, was shot very documentary-like — with almost kind of a long-lens look — of flying to work at dawn in pollution and traffic, and having the odd fellow who's the hotrodder spin out of his lane and butt in front of you and peel off. And people in the spinners mumbling under their breath and waving at each other and that sort of thing. So the feeling we were trying to get across was that this is not extraordinary to these people, any more than freeway driving is in Los Angeles. This is their environment, and they expect to see it that way. So, with the exception of the opening where we have a kind of grand approach to the Tyrell Corporation pyramids, we tried not to make it look spectacular, but just crowded and congested and smoky and rainy."

The last major item on the effects docket was the giant advertising blimp seen drifting languorously over the city from time to time. It was also among the last elements to be incorporated into the script. "The blimp is an extension of media advertising," said Scott, "and in a way, it's also kind of a throwback to my childhood during the second World War. My family was living in a suburb of London, and we had these barrage balloons flying overhead. In fact, there was a whole line of them on cables right across the southern seaboard in kind of a triangular wedge leading into London; and the idea was that the buzz bombs and the Messerschmitts would fly into these cables and be brought down or deflected off course before they could get to the city. I remember one of the balloons burst one night and settled over our house, and we woke up the next morning and thought it was still dark. So all that experience was still in the back of my mind; and I thought maybe in the future we might get back to that idea as an advertising medium. Already they're talking about moving back to the old-fashioned idea of using blimps to carry cargo and passengers — for fuel reasons, mainly. So you could have a blimp that's maybe four hundred feet long, with a major screen on it that's two hundred feet across and a couple others a hundred feet each — that's a lot of advertising power, especially if it's really visual. They'd be anchored to the ground, and they'd slowly drift about like a big whale and they'd cover maybe twelve

All the matte paintings were designed by Syd Mead. Working directly over photographic prints derived from the live-action photography, Mead prepared detailed watercolor renderings which were approved by Ridley Scott and then followed precisely. Though his designs generally met with no resistance, Mead's first attempt at one rooftop scene was rejected because it looked too open. / He then prepared a more claustrophobic alternate which was approved and eventually translated into a matte painting by Rocco Gioffre. / Gioffre at work on the rooftop painting. / Matte assistant Michelle Moen traces a rotoscope projection of the building so a matte can be generated for adding smoke and rain effects.

square miles — which is a lot when you consider the population density, but you'd probably still need twenty or thirty of them across a city of fifty or sixty million people."

"The initial idea," said Douglas Trumbull, "was that the blimp would be this sort of big, dark shape that on the storyboard was drawn to look like a regular blimp with some kind of big illuminated signs on the body — very much like the Goodyear blimp. *We* thought, though, that the blimp ought to be a really strange-looking contraption, with big flat signs on it at various angles and a few lights on board. Ridley liked that approach, and so that's the way we did it. It was always supposed to be just kind of a background thing; but as it turned out, Ridley really fell in love with that blimp and kept ordering up more and more shots. And then he decided he wanted it to be bigger. Well, one of the things you tend to resort to to get scale is lots of tiny little lights. Lights on a miniature tend to look like windows; and therefore, if a little point of light looks like a window, then the overall shape must be very big. So Ridley asked for lots of little lights to be added to the blimp, plus a lot of antennas and stuff. As a result, it ended up looking kind of like a sleazy mothership — which the cognoscenti of the special effects business are probably going to have a good laugh over."

Shortly before he left the project, Wayne Smith had put together a small foam study mockup of the blimp as it was conceived at the time. "Originally, it was supposed to be just a throwaway type thing," said Mark Stetson, "to be seen in the background a few times, and that was it. So we ended up putting it off and putting it off; and aside from Wayne's foam and paper mockup, we didn't put any more design effort into it at all for quite a long time. Then, after Bill George had gotten all his other vehicles done, he came to me and asked if I wanted him to build the blimp. I said sure. Aside from the fact that it was supposed to carry advertising signs and look kind of puffy and overinflated, we didn't have a whole lot to go on. And at first we tried a number of things that just weren't working. We tried making up a series of masonite templates, assembling them into kind of an x-y grid, and then stretching a sheet of styrene over the top and heating it to see if it would drape over this template grid into the form that we wanted. It didn't. We tried it with heat and air, and that didn't work either. We tried it with heat on wet rags to push it out and cool it into place, and it *still* didn't work."

"The final form," Bill George explained, "was fabricated by first building a box with the symmetrical centerline cut in the top. Curved ribs were then added to the inside. So essentially, what it ended up being was a negative skeleton of the intended shape. Next, a thin sheet of surgical neoprene rubber was stretched over the centerline hole in the top, and then filled with wet plaster. The weight of the plaster ballooned the latex between the ribs, spontaneously creating the inflated look. The blimp shape was about three feet long and ended up holding over a hundred pounds of plaster. And there were three of us, mixing plaster with our hands and filling it in, sure that at any moment the over-stretched latex would burst and spill wet plaster all over us.

Ridley Scott coaches Harrison Ford for the sequence in which Deckard clings perilously from the edge of a skyscraper. / For the master matte shot — since Deckard was to dangle directly over the painted urban canyon — a white card was placed behind Ford so a functional traveling matte could be extracted from the production photography. The painting itself was begun by Rocco Gioffre and completed by Matthew Yuricich. A moving spinner was photographed as a still transparency, and then matted into the distance. / Animation cameraman Glenn Campbell prepares to rotoscope a shot on the animation stand. / Richard Yuricich — chief architect of the EEG matte system — advises Ridley Scott on a live-action matte shot setup.

CINEFEX 9 ▶ 65

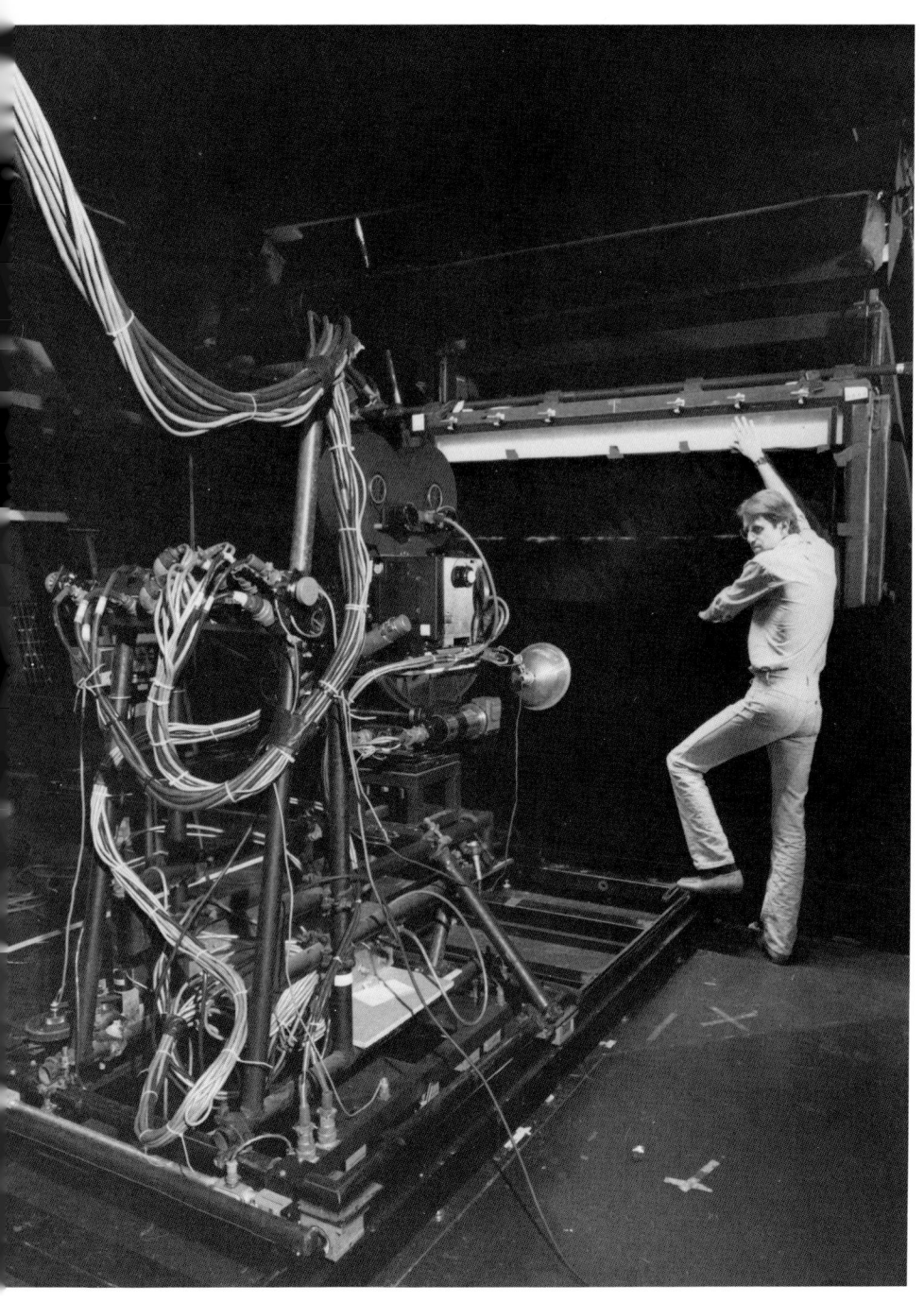

Fortunately it didn't, but I got so excited because it was working that I didn't notice the plaster had hardened on my forearms. The process may seem like a lot of trouble, but the gentle intersecting curves would have taken weeks to sculpt or carve."

"We let the plaster set up for a few days," Mark Stetson continued, "and then turned it upside-down and poured a thick rubber mold over it — just a throwaway — and got two quick castings out of it and slapped the thing together. At that point, Ridley reviewed it for the first time, and he was really kind of enchanted with it. But he started asking for lots of changes — which I think meant that he really liked it. The advertising projection screens were changed. We added a bunch of bristling antennas around the outside, and lots of fiber optic lights. Mike McMillen and Rick Guttierez were working on it at that point, and Mike came up with a little chopper wheel between the fiber optic bundle and the light source so the little lights would flicker and blink. With the optics spread out across the blimp body and this flickering chopper wheel going, it was really starting to look pretty interesting. We presented it to Ridley again, and he liked it even better this time — but he wanted still more changes. For one thing, he wanted to change the scale so it would look twice as big. So we added more lights and detail pieces and built a new cabin. Dave Dryer also liked it a lot and had some of his own changes he wanted made. So it really went through three full generations of construction before it finally got on camera." By this time, the old Army-surplus look that was the basis of the original concept had given way to something altogether different — summed up rather aptly by the model shop crew who collectively dubbed it the "mother-blimp."

At first it was intended that the black screens on which the advertising would appear would remain in place at all times. However, once the blimp made its way into the smoke room and began undergoing film tests, David Dryer devised a new approach. "Rather than having some kind of an opaque screen, we decided to have only a border, and nothing tangible within. Then, when it was energized and the advertising message appeared, it would do so kind of magically — almost from nowhere. The image would be kind of semitransparent and it would sputter a bit and zap on like some sort of holographic television. We did that by filming the fill-light passes and the practical light passes without the screen in place. Then, for the commercial pass, we'd insert a silk screen into that area and project our off-world footage — or whatever else the shot called for — onto that, so it seemed to exist in space within that border in front of the blimp." As they had with the spinners, Don Baker and Tim McHugh accomplished most of the actual blimp photography.

Although the blimp appears in several places throughout the film, one of the most interesting shots was derived from a location shoot at the Bradbury Building in downtown Los Angeles. The historic structure — built in 1893 — served as genetics designer Sebastian's apartment house in the film, and an exterior scene when Deckard enters revealed the blimp drifting overhead. Inside, the building featured an open atrium with elegant staircases, open-cage elevators and a glass dome ceiling several stories up. To best make use of the splendid locale, it was decided to introduce a shot in which Deckard glances up and sees the blimp through the dome. A traditional approach would have entailed photographing a film plate inside the building and then trying to insert the blimp optically into the open areas. In this case, however, the dome was broken up by individually-framed panes of glass that would have complicated the matting process immeasurably. Also, since the blimp was equipped with an array of xenon post scanners that could throw miniature searchlight-type beams in any direction, if one were to sweep over the building below, its shaft of light should logically be fractured by the latticework — which would not happen if the image was simply matted in.

"As it turned out," said Virgil Mirano, "the most economical and direct way of dealing with the problem was to shoot a still. So I went down there one night when everything was going on outside, and I set up my camera and took the shot. It was ideal, in a way, because it didn't tie up the whole crew and it didn't impede the production. Plus with a still, of course, you have time on your hands with regards to exposures. So you can get maximum depth of field, largest angle of view with a variety of lenses, and utilize existing lighting. That still was then blown up to a very large Ektacolor print which was mounted with spray adhesive onto one of the thick pieces of matte painting glass. But since prints tend to be translucent, we first had to apply an opaque backing to the glass. Once the print was mounted, John Wash went in and very precisely cut out all the window areas on the print so there was just clear glass behind them. Then, during the actual photography, the matte glass was locked down to the base upon which the camera itself was mounted. So as the camera moved along the track under motion control, the cutout photographic print moved right along with it. The blimp, meanwhile, was in a fixed position — but on film, of course, it appears to be passing overhead, moving behind the grillwork on this Victorian-style elevator, as well as all the individual little skylight elements. It's quite a dramatic shot, especially when those post scanners sweep across the lines on the print and you get this wonderful spread as the beam penetrates the haze."

In keeping with Ridley Scott's passion for "layering" his special effects imagery, many of the *Blade Runner* shots feature incidental atmospheric elements intended for execution by the animation department — which consisted primarily of supervisor John Wash and cameraman Glenn Campbell. "Vehicles were a big part of the picture," said Wash, "and in addition to the models that were shot on the stages, we produced a lot of elements like running lights and flashing strobe lights on vehicles that are traveling way off in the distance, just to create a greater density to the look of the megalopolis." Glenn Campbell found such elements to be a great enhancement to the overall ambience. "Most cities-of-the-future films are very cold and sterile," he cited. "You don't really get the feeling that people are living there. In the foreground, they'll throw in a couple of extras wearing Roman togas, and that's about it. In *this* film, you have a city where people are on the move — guys going to work, ladies going off grocery shopping, dropping the kids off at school. There're cars way out there in west Hell, and traffic jams — things like that."

The primary piece of hardware in the EEG animation department is a lone Oxberry animation stand, adapted for the 65mm format and topped by an old Todd-AO bipack camera. "It had the big old square-type 65mm magazines," said the six-foot-five-inch Campbell, "and they were really heavy. So if you used it like a normal animation stand, you'd have registration problems, because once you took the magazine off, the camera would go, 'Aw geez, thanks,' and straighten up. And when it did, you'd lose everything you'd just roto'd. So we never took the magazines off the camera. We down-loaded from the camera stand with lights out and the door closed. In fact, I think that's why they hired me. I'm the only one tall enough to reach up there and thread it without killing myself on a ladder."

"Most of what we did on the animation stand was pretty simple stuff," said John Wash. "In some of the matte paintings, we wanted to have big streams of traffic in the background — like there were controlled air lanes full of spinners moving in both directions — and those were very easily done with a slot gag on the Oxberry. Most of them were so far away that they were just points of light, so we had one group of lines that defined the traffic pattern that was going horizontally, and then another group of lines that were open vertically and were keyed to each little dot of light on the car. So they were colored with different gels and some ND (neutral density) stuff to make different headlights brighter or dimmer, or make certain taillights redder. Then, just by moving that up and down against the traffic lane, you'd get this series of traveling lights. To add to the complexity, we'd do different passes at different speeds to make it look like some cars were overtaking others. We also used slot gags in many of the painted buildings off in the distance to put in little shimmering points of light that helped create a convincing representation of buildings seen through heat waves or atmospheric haze."

Although the Oxberry was also of considerable use on such standard requirements as the Tyrell office sun, straight-line laser zaps and lightning bolts, most of the animation effects involved inserting distant spinners — either two-dimensional transparencies or simple point-light sources — into frequently moving background plates. While such shots *could* be plotted out manually on an animation stand, the Oxberry in use at EEG was handicapped in that it did not have rotation capability. Also, like other traditional stands, it operated on a move-and-shoot basis, which precluded the incorporation of natural blur. As a result, it was decided the spinner animation should be done on EEG's exclusive Compsy system — a servo-drive computerized multiplane system first employed on *Star Trek – The Motion Picture* to produce the diaphanous, multilayered V'ger cloud passage, the streaking *Enterprise* for the wormhole sequence, and numerous multiplane star effects. Although its full

Numerous distant spinner elements were created on EEG's exclusive Compsy system — a computerized multiplane system which also functions as a motion controlled horizontal animation stand. Tech director Richard Hollander employed the system extensively to help plot camera moves used on previously photographed cityscape and pyramid miniatures, and then translate those moves onto a two-dimensional graphic arts plane. As a result, he was able to program shots which allowed for the straight-line insertion of backlit spinner transparencies and tiny moving light sources into constantly shifting three-dimensional background imagery.

capabilities have yet to be tapped, at its very simplest, the Compsy system can be thought of as a highly-sophisticated horizontal animation stand — basically a large motorized graphic arts plane with a motion-controlled camera mounted perpendicular to it on a thirty-six-foot track.

For the moving camera scenes requiring later animation work, the stage crews shot a final pass in each miniature setup solely to help orient the animators. "They'd put Xs of white tape at various points around the set," said John Wash, "both close to the camera and far away — and then they'd do a film run that was exactly the same as the production shot. From that we were able to plot, very precisely, just how the camera was moving during the course of the shot. We did that by rotoscoping the motion control model move on Compsy and figuring out the velocities and tracks of the various items. Then we had to try to fit a curve to that track that we could use in shooting our two-dimensional artwork. Fortunately, Richard Hollander was able to come up with the software to plot those moves very quickly, and as a result we were able to get a lot of nice curving moves and match up groups of spinners to a model shot where the camera is moving and yet these animated spinners would be flying along in proper registration, disappearing behind buildings and coming around the other side. Even then, though, it required a degree of experimentation — shooting passes on black-and-white film, having them processed, and then bipacking them on the Moviola to see just how they turned out."

"On one of the shots," recalled Compsy tech director Richard Hollander, "I had to match a traffic lane that physically existed in the model. But the camera moved in on the model, so you couldn't just plot two points and have traffic go between those because the line of travel was changing as time went on. But by using the camera system as kind of a huge, hand-held calculator, I was able to figure out just what path these things would run as time went on in the scene. So in effect, what I did was model 3-D space as though it were a bar, and then travel little lights down this hypothetical bar so the perspective changes were all the same. The effect's not exactly what you'd call a bomb-blaster, but it was pretty interesting nonetheless. Very subtle."

In many ways, it was the subtlety that appealed most to John Wash. "I did mostly advertising work before *Blade Runner*," he explained, "and inevitably you'd have your clients hammering at you for large, bombastic, flared-out images. So to me, it was kind of intriguing to be involved in a project where we had to use a really light touch and just make things look very realistic and very convincing."

Once the appropriate moves had been plotted and stored in Compsy's memory, it was time to shoot the actual spinner imagery that would be incorporated into the shot. "We tried various different things for the distant light effects," said Hollander. "What we basically wanted was a small white light and then a blinking red light for each spinner. The first thing we tried was backlighting a small hole, but that ended up not looking very good. It spread out for some odd reason and was just too wide of a source. What we finally ended up using — believe it or not — was just the head of a pin, painted white and frontlit on black velvet. That was shot from about fifteen feet away and provided a really nice point source. The blinking red light, though, we wanted to be stronger and brighter; so that was done as a separate pass with a tiny wheat bulb behind a small hole in the artwork, with a gel in the camera. Some of the shots had three or four of these little spinner things in the background — flying around at different speeds and blinking at different times — but once it was set up, the whole process was pretty much automatic. In fact, one of the really nice things about Compsy is that you don't even have to be there. The system will finish its run and then turn itself off and wait for you to set up the next one. At one point I even got tired of going in and out of the room to see if it was done, so I hooked it up to a pager unit and programmed it to beep me when it was finished. You can't get much more automatic than that."

Not all of the Compsy spinners were mere light sources, however. The high-angle down-shot of Rachael crossing the intersection, for example, called for several vehicles to traverse the painted underpasses beneath the real street. "In that case," said John Wash, "there were no perspective changes, and the moves were so simple that it was easier for *us* to shoot it than it was to do it as a model shot on the stage. Virgil Mirano and I shot four-by-five color transparencies of some of the models in correct perspective, and then we shot those backlit on Compsy so they seemed to be moving through the scene. On separate passes, we shot little headlights through a scratch filter to give them a diffused look; and we also did some shadow passes against the roadway they were traveling on. And, of course, we had to do a holdout matte to be used by optical in compositing the shot."

A special effects project of any magnitude carries with it many potential pitfalls — not all of them strictly related to putting images on film. With any given shot consisting of a dozen or more separate film elements — some of which may have required several takes — an effects facility can quickly flounder if careful attention is not paid to keeping track of each and every piece of film. At EEG, that responsibility lies with Jack Hinkle. "When I first came to work for Richard and Doug six years ago, if they needed something, it took them three or four days to find it. After a couple of months, I think I was earning them more than my salary just in time savings." Although officially designated as lab liaison, Hinkle's duties are wide-ranging. "Every piece of film that's shot in this facility comes direct to me from the cameras. I push it through the lab; and when it comes back I catalog it by day, roll, scene, key number and camera — which could be Oxberry, Stage One, matte camera, whatever. Then I file the film away, and if someone comes to me and says, 'I need so-and-so,' all they have to do is give me a date or a slate number or almost anything, and I can lay my hands on it right away. Then, after we've got everything we need for a given shot, I'll pull all the elements and write up an order to our optical department so

The advertising blimp as originally conceived and constructed by Bill George — who signed it with his initials and birthdate. Shortly after it was completed, the concept changed and numerous additions and refinements were incorporated, primarily to make it look bigger. / Mike McMillen makes a voltage check on the fiber optic light circuits. / Fully composited, the blimp passes quietly over the miniature cityscape.

CINEFEX 9 ► 69

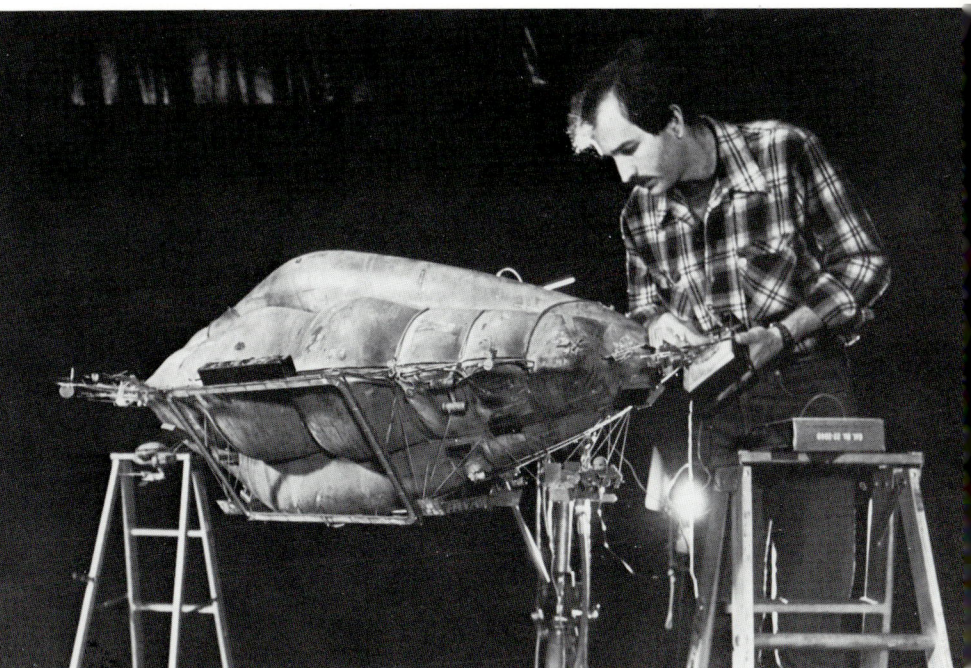

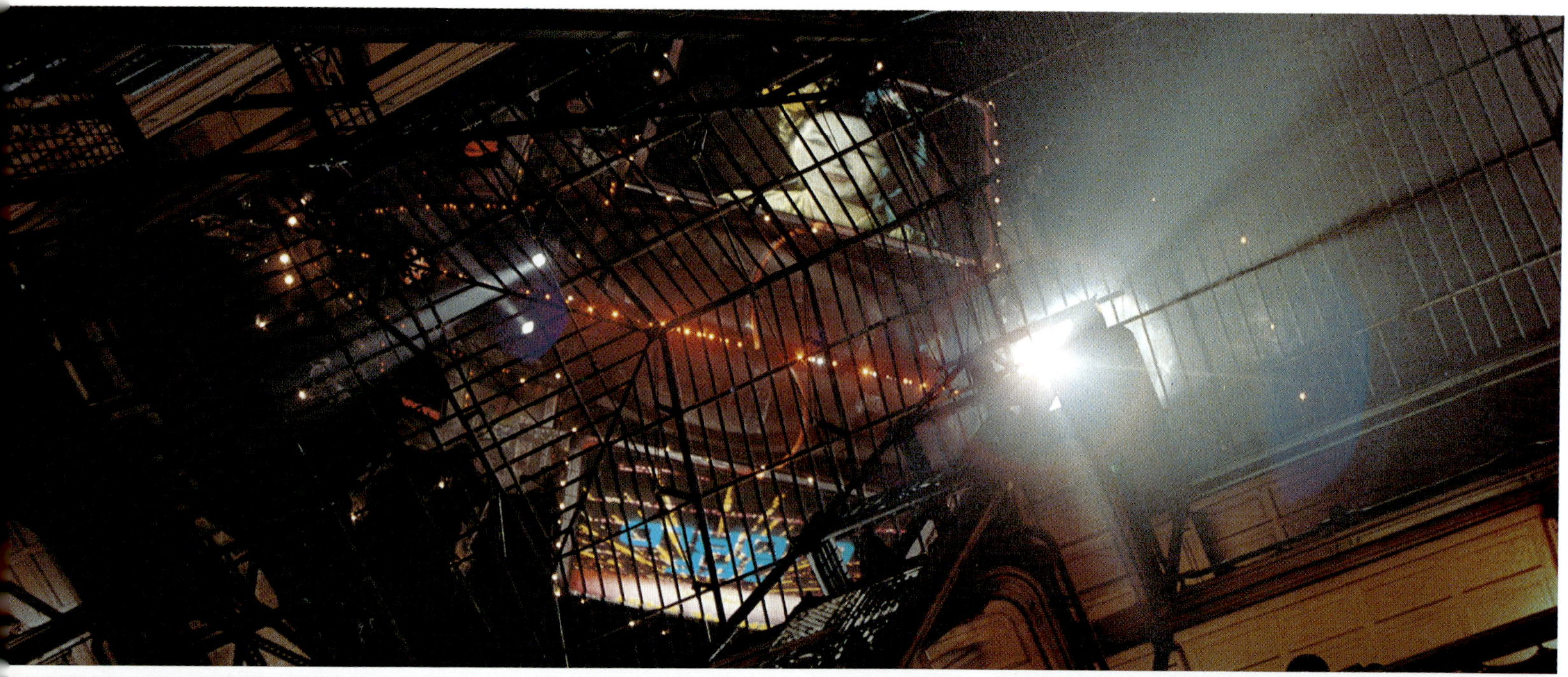

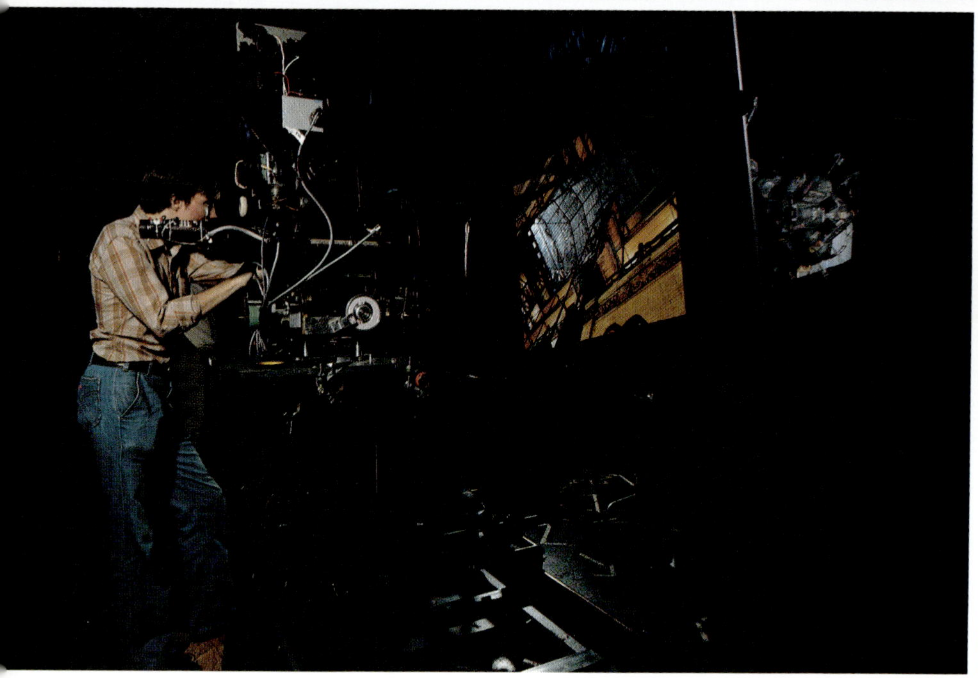

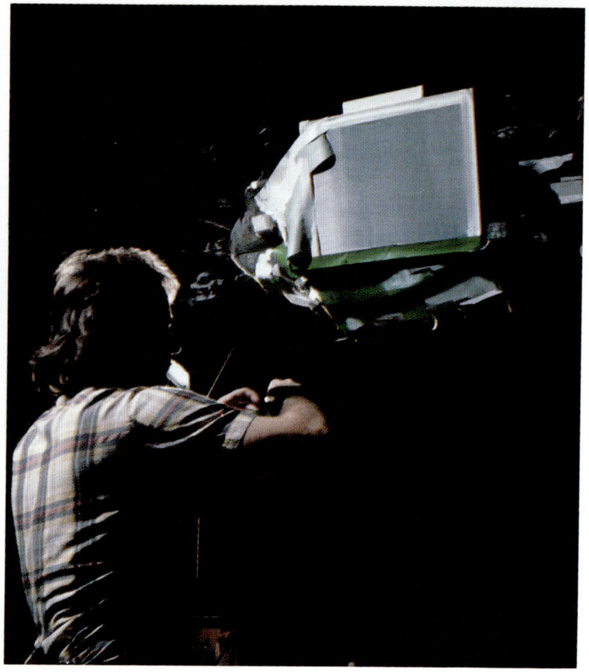

they can start putting them together."

Just exactly how they should be put together — in terms of element placement, timing and so on — was not always readily apparent, but it was up to David Dryer to take a first stab at it. His elections were recorded in Jack Hinkle's production log and then relayed to the optical department. After a precomposite was made, it would be studied exhaustively in the screening room, and if changes were deemed necessary, Hinkle would thread it up on a synchronizer in the editing room so that Dryer could examine it more minutely against a field chart. Sometimes a spinner would be made to enter a few frames later in the shot, or it might be flopped, or repositioned by a field or two — whatever. Hinkle meanwhile, recorded the specific frame counts and positioning instructions — which he then relayed to the optical department for the next composite attempt. The extent of the cumulative record-keeping involved can be evidenced in the fact that some fifteen to twenty pages of notes, diagrams and miscellaneous log entries were required for just about every effects shot in the film.

A shorthand version of the master log graced the crowded walls of David Dryer's office in the form of individual continuity sheets which outlined the status of each shot in progress. Initially, each sheet contained a storyboard sketch of the proposed scene, along with sufficient room beneath to annotate completion of its various elements. Then, as the film elements began coming in, the sketches were overlaid with color xerox frame enlargements rendered directly from the 65mm workprint. When all the elements were shot and the final composite approved, a large red dot was applied to signify completion.

By the time the effects unit wrapped, the original thirty-eight shots budgeted for the film had blossomed to more than ninety — which in the editorial phase were cut back to about sixty-five. "They were nice shots," Richard Yuricich commented, "but Ridley used even the effects as an editorial piece, and some of them wound up in the trash." Even so, at $3.5 million, the overall effects package was still a bargain when compared to the original budget estimates. "As we saw it," said Douglas Trumbull, "our job was to demonstrate to our producers and to the rest of the movie community that the business of special effects can be operated *as* a business — that there *is* a way to plan how much it'll cost and how long it'll take and how it can be done, that it doesn't have to be a big mystery and it doesn't have to go out of control. And we're trying to develop a reputation of studios and executives and producers being able to trust us to advise them correctly, and not make a big hoopla out of it and not try to put up a lot of flak and difficulties for them."

"We look upon the shop as nothing more than a giant Erector set," Richard Yuricich added. "We have cameras and motion control devices and all kinds of specialized equipment — but they're nothing but tools, and tools will never replace the artist. What makes it all come together is the people who work here. In many ways we're like an artist's palette, and what comes out is a reflection of the artistry that goes in. *Blade Runner* was Ridley Scott's movie all the way — even more so, I think, than Stanley Kubrick's *2001*. He was the driving force. Everything was done the way *Ridley* wanted, and he really put our equipment and our people through their paces. But the crew here liked him and admired him and rose to the challenge. And I think the results are there on the screen."

Clearly, *Blade Runner* is a cornucopia of special effects, but one whose perceptual treats have been carefully subordinated to the overall thrust of the film. As a result, Ridley Scott — like many other directors — chafes even at the thought that his work might be labeled an "effects" film, as though its only function were that of providing a showcase for visual pyrotechnics. "I think probably it was the way I was brought up, but effects movies — in the Fifties and Sixties — were always somehow slightly tainted, if you know what I mean. They were kind of grouped together with sex movies and things like that that just weren't quite the right thing to go and see. So I never went to any. The only films I used to see that involved effects were some of the better ones that came out on television — The Day the Earth Stood Still and things like that. And I think it was that sort of odd detachment which kept most directors away from effects — as though they were thinking: 'Well, do I really want to get into this? Because maybe I'm going to be slightly discolored as well.' I think the first *real* film — which is the obvious one — that really made effects respectable was *2001*. Prior to that, I had never really seen an effects film that *worked* on every level — where there was a reality to everything and the whole proscenium of the film was real. As soon as that happened, it opened up my eyes and I realized that at some point in time I would get into effects movies — even though I hate the term. But I think directors are certainly beginning to realize that effects are just part and parcel of making a film. It just opens up the whole platform. It's like horror films or science fiction or whatever — as soon as the classy ones get made, they become respectable. And it increases your scope; it increases the theatre within which you can work. For a long time, I think subjects were stagnating — police films, cowboy films, love stories, thrillers. Somebody once said there are only seven stories in the world anyhow. But within *all* the genres, I think there was stagnation to a degree. So now, instead of doing a police story set in New York, why not open it up and do it somewhere else — some other time, some other place? All it's really doing is laying demands on your imagination. The trick really is integrating the environment into the story. You don't just write a screenplay with an effects shot here, an effects shot there. You have to set that environment way back into the script; and the more integrated it can be, the better. Effects just help you bring it out."

Blade Runner *photographs copyright © 1982 by The Ladd Company. All rights reserved. Special effects unit still photography by Virgil Mirano. Additional photography by Mark Stetson and Bill George. Special thanks to Jeff Walker.*

A point-of-view shot as Deckard enters Sebastian's apartment house and glances up through the glass-roofed atrium at the blimp passing overhead. / To achieve the effect, a still photograph taken inside the Bradbury Building location was mounted on a thick pane of glass, and then all the window areas were carefully cut out. The glass, in turn, was mounted onto the camera rig so that it moved as the camera did. The blimp, therefore, remained stationary behind it, but still appeared to be drifting by. Assistant cameraman Tim McHugh lines up the shot. / Simulated video images on the blimp were projected onto a silk screen to convey an electronic look. Pat Van Auken positions and masks the screen, which was included in the shot only during the separate commercial pass.

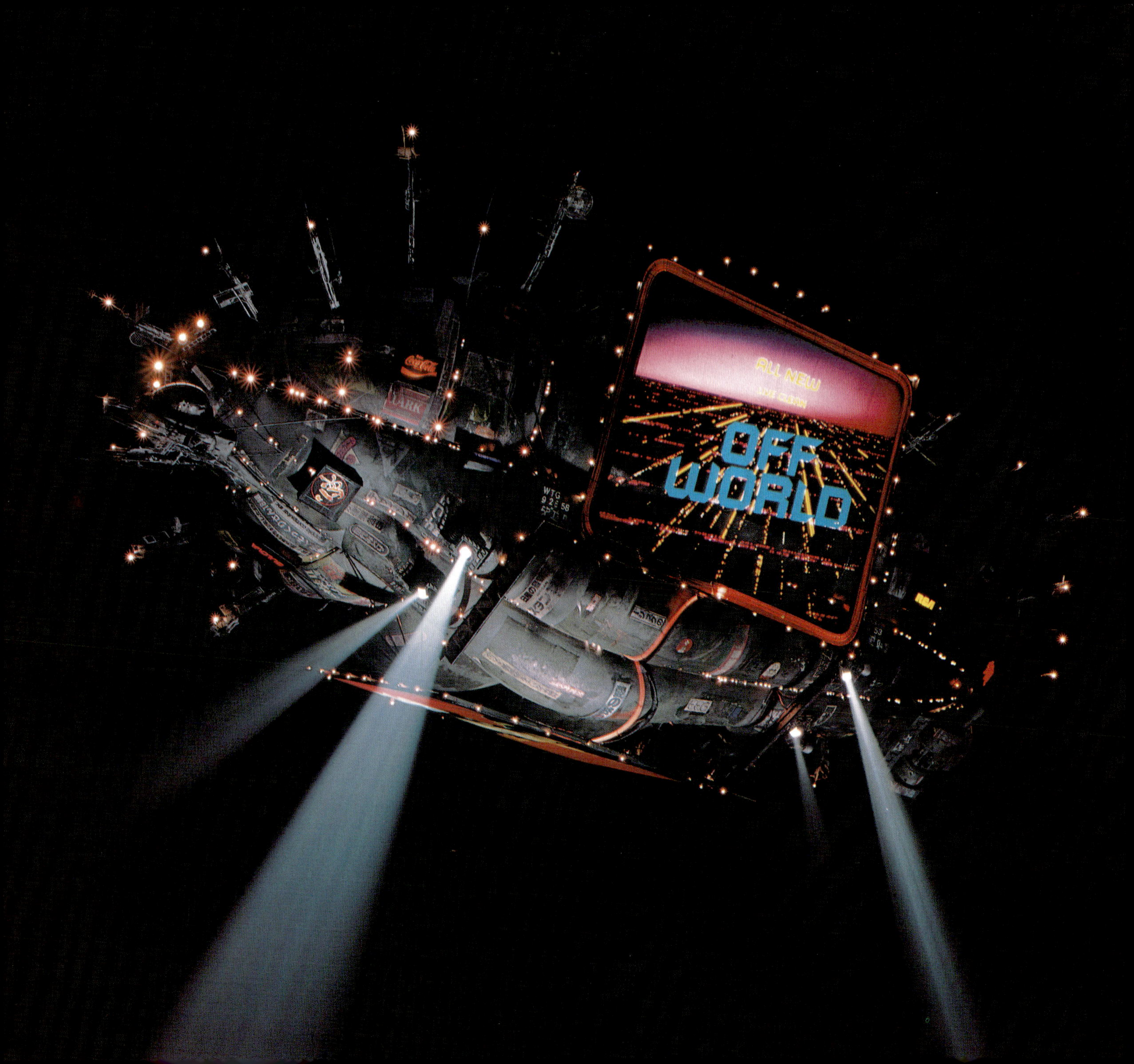
ALL NEW
OFF
WORLD

cinefex

20 years of unsurpassed special effects coverage

www.cinefex.com